CLINTON ROSSITER

---•---

The
Political Thought
of the
American Revolution

---•---

A HARVEST BOOK

Harcourt, Brace & World, Inc.

NEW YORK

*L*ook back, therefore, with reverence look back to the times of ancient virtue and renown. Look back to the mighty purposes which your fathers had in view, when they traversed a vast ocean, and planted this land. Recal to your minds their labours, their toils, their perseverance, and let their divine spirit animate you in all your actions.

Look forward also to distant posterity. Figure to yourselves millions and millions to spring from your loins, who may be born *freemen* or *slaves,* as Heaven shall now approve or reject your councils. Think, that on you may depend, whether this great country, in ages hence, shall be filled and adorned with a virtuous and inlightened people; enjoying *Liberty* and all its concomitant blessings . . . or covered with a race of men more contemptible than the savages that roam the wilderness.

—REV. WILLIAM SMITH, 1775

Preface

MY INTENTION in publishing this revised version of Part III of *Seedtime of the Republic* is to present the essential political thought of the American Revolution within the covers of one small book.

Whether the principles of the men who carried us from servitude to independence and beyond to the edge of glory are fully viable in an America of automation and nuclear energy is a question open to debate. Whether they can be made fully intelligible to a world in large parts of which our kind of liberty has never been known or even imagined is a question to which the answer is very probably "no." Since we cannot, alas, expect the revolutions of this age to take ours as a model, in particular to be as reluctant, limited, measured, self-generating, and, for that matter, successful, we cannot expect the men who lead them to think and behave, as did our founding fathers, like Englishmen in the wilderness. The "self-evident truths" of 1776, unless they are twisted out of shape or ripped out of context, can never have the same appeal to the new nations of Asia and Africa in the twentieth century that they did to the new nation of North America in the eighteenth.

At the same time, the principles of the American Revolution are well worth studying, whether by men who enjoy freedom or men who aspire to it. The Revolution was, after all, one of the longest and surest strides the world has ever taken toward the grand goal of "liberty for all mankind," and no men of good will, even those men who define liberty almost exclusively in terms of economic development and national independence, can afford to be ignorant of the faith that animated Washington, Franklin, Jefferson, Hamilton, Dickinson, Wilson, the Lees, and the Adamses. As aspiration, if not as description or prescription, the political thought of the Revolution has the ring both of eternity and universality.

For these reasons, and for the added reason that the American Revolution, whatever its influence and relevance, was an astonishing and encouraging event of history, I have thought it important to present this survey of the noble political philosophy that vindicated the campaign of resistance to British coercion (1765-1775), the final lunge toward independence (1775-1776), and the establishment of the new state governments (1776-1780). In the pages that follow I have paid particular attention to the first of these periods. I have done this in obedience to the plain truth that the intellectual history of the Revolution is largely confined to the years between the passage of the Stamp Act and the resolution for independence. It was in this period that the American colonists carried on their critical debates, proclaimed their central ideas, and reached their one truly revolutionary decision: to strike out on their own as a republic. If the years under Washington were those that tried men's souls, the years under Samuel Adams were those that searched their minds.

The intellectual history of this great event can be narrowed in subject matter as well as in time, for it is chiefly a history of political ideas. The announced purpose of the Americans was to dissolve the political bands that had connected them with England. The central problem of the decade was largely political in nature, and the search for solutions was pushed along political lines. Political thought rather than economic, religious, or social thought was the chief beneficiary of the outpouring of speeches, sermons, letters, resolves, and pamphlets that greeted each new move of the British ministry.

Two final points before we "look back . . . to the times of ancient virtue and renown." First, I have done my best to let the men of the Revolution, both great and small, speak for themselves. I hope it will be understood that the apparently inordinate length of some of the excerpts from pamphlets, sermons, and documents in these pages is a product of design and not of dereliction. Second, I have also made a special effort to bring a reasonable amount of order to a political philosophy marked by charming disorder. The result, I think, is a book that should leave no doubt in the mind of anyone who reads it carefully about the ideas our founding fathers meant to recommend to "the opinions of mankind." To those ideas we continue to pay—or so at least we like to boast—the devotion of both veneration and imitation. If our devotion is to be intelligent, we must all know more exactly what the ideas were. Ignorance has no place in a philosophy of liberty.

CLINTON ROSSITER

Ithaca, New York
June, 1963

Contents

For an extensive bibliographical and documentary annotation of these chapters, see pages 453-456, 518-538 of *Seedtime of the Republic*.

One

---◆---

THE CONTEXT OF REVOLUTIONARY
POLITICAL THOUGHT

---◆---

*I*f ever a body of ideas was a product of history, a conspicuously successful servant of the practical purposes of determined men, it was the political thought of the American Revolution. One begins a study of this justly famous body of ideas by recognizing the close affinity of fact and principle, of practical purpose and philosophical justification, in the minds of the men who made the Revolution. Let us therefore turn first to a survey of the spokesmen, agencies, purposes, and characteristics of political writing in the years of struggle and decision between 1765 and 1780, and let us also say something about the sources upon which the Americans drew for comfort and inspiration. Separated from this historical context, the political thought of the Revolution is a warmed-over hash of ancient platitudes; kept within this context, it is a magnificent invocation of first principles in support of human liberty and constitutional government.

The American Spokesmen

THE POLITICAL PRINCIPLES of the Revolution were so unsophisticated in expression and inclusive in appeal as to seem a declaration of faith rather than a body of theory. The uniquely popular nature of these principles is apparent in the status and calling of the men who expounded them to the people. The spokesmen of the American cause arose from every class and occupation. The natural leaders of all groups and classes joined in political argument and, to a greater or lesser degree, in the common American practice of "recurring to first principles." Tavern-keeper, cartman, and village wit stood as ready to declaim on internal taxation and the social compact as John Adams or James Otis.

Unfortunately for the historian of ideas, few tavern-keepers or village wits ever broke into print. At least one good reason for this state of affairs was that they had no need to speak out to a larger audience. Every possible variation of the reigning faith had already found expression in the writings of political and religious leaders of the upper and middle classes, and the average man was content to echo the brave assertions of his delegate or minister. Political thought in the Revolutionary period was popular in the sense that a group of articulate leaders prophesied to the people, and that the people made these prophecies their own.

The remembered leaders in political thought and argument were, with few exceptions, men active in the affairs of town or colony, or in the slowly forming continental union. The largest group consisted of lawyers, the next largest of preachers, a third of merchants and planters. Whatever their first calling, their second was politics and political speculation. Scarcely a figure of importance to the political historian is any less important to the historian of ideas. This fact, of course, gave the public writing of the period some of its most obvious characteristics—its urgency, simplicity, and broad appeal, its willingness to recur to first principles but not to probe them. At least three men active in the early years of the Revolution could have become first-rate political theorists in the universal sense of the term, but the mere mention of their names—Thomas Jefferson, John Adams, and James Wilson—reveals why they never had a chance. The period was ill-designed for the kind of speculation in which each of these men was later to engage.

The men from whom we shall be hearing through all these pages make up a virtually complete roster of the political thinkers of the American Revolution. The chief spokesmen in secular affairs, most of them lawyers from the upper or upper-middle class, were Jefferson, Benjamin Franklin, Samuel Adams, John Adams, Wilson, Richard Bland, James Otis, John Dickinson, Theophilus Parsons, Alexander Hamilton, George Mason, and

Thomas Paine. Slightly less important as individual thinkers but collectively an eminent array of orators and pamphleteers were Josiah Quincy, Patrick Henry, Oxenbridge Thacher, Daniel Dulany, Joseph Hawley, William Henry Drayton, Stephen Hopkins, the three Lee brothers of Virginia, William Livingston, Samuel Chase, James Iredell, Joseph Warren, John Hancock, Benjamin Church, Silas Downer, James Bowdoin, David Ramsay, George Wythe, and Edward Bancroft. Men like Thomas Mifflin, Joseph Reed, Thomas Dawes, James Lovell, and those staunch Whig publishers John Holt of the *New-York Journal* and Isaiah Thomas of the *Massachusetts Spy* could be added to this list without detracting one bit from its luster.

Rev. William Gordon of Roxbury began a sermon in December, 1774, with these words of apology and admonition:

> The pulpit is devoted, in general, to more important purposes than the fate of kingdoms, or the civil rights of human nature, being intended to recover men from the slavery of sin and Satan, to point out their escape from future misery through faith in a crucified Jesus, and to assist them in their preparations for an eternal blessedness. But still there are special times and seasons when it may treat of politics.

The Revolution was just such a special time and season. The clergy not only treated of politics but played the game as well. A loyalist writing in 1774 attested the importance of the New England ministers to the patriot cause in these angry words:

> It is an indubitable fact that previous to and during all these acts of violence, committed in the Colonies, especially to the eastward, the Presbyterian pulpits groaned with the

most wicked, malicious and inflammatory harangues, pronounced by the favourite orators amongst that sect, spiriting their godly hearers to the most violent opposition to Government; persuading them that the intention of Government was to rule them with a rod of iron, and to make them all slaves; and assuring them that if they would rise as one man to oppose those arbitrary schemes, *God* would assist them to sweep away every *ministerial tool,* (the amiable name these wretches are pleased to bestow on the professors of the Church) from the face of the earth; that now was the time to strike, whilst Government at home was afraid of them; together with a long string of such seditious stuff, well calculated to impose on the poor devils their hearers, and make them run into every degree of extravagance and folly.

The work of the clergy as leaders of political thought was equally impressive. Had ministers been the only spokesmen of the American cause, had Jefferson, the Adamses, and Otis never appeared in print, the political thought of the Revolution would have followed almost exactly the same line—with perhaps a little more mention of God, but certainly no less of John Locke. In the sermons of the patriot ministers, who were responsible for fully one third of the total output of political thought in these years, we find expressed every possible refinement of the reigning secular faith. The leading thinkers among the ministers, for the most part sons of the Puritan churches, were Jonathan Mayhew, Charles Chauncy, Samuel Cooper, Stephen Johnson, Jonas Clarke, Samuel Webster, and Samuel Cooke. A step behind this select band of prophets was a small army— "the black Regiment," as Peter Oliver labeled it—of staunch expounders of English and natural rights: William Gordon, Samuel West, Samuel Langdon, Judah

Champion, Ebenezer Devotion, Simeon Howard, Amos Adams, John Cleaveland, Phillips Payson, Isaac Skillman, John Allen, Thomas Allen, Gad Hitchcock, John Tucker, Charles Turner, Ebenezer Bridge, Eliphalet Williams, Edward Barnard, Jason Haven, Samuel Lockwood, and literally hundreds of others hardly less skilled than Mayhew or Cooper in expounding the doctrines of resistance, unalienable rights, and consent.

Outside New England the clergy was less accustomed to find its way into print on political matters, but such names as John Witherspoon, William Smith, Jacob Duché, John Joachim Zubly, John Hurt, and William Tennent are evidence that there, too, men of God were keen participants in political argument. The incidence of loyalist ministers was somewhat higher in colonies where the Church of England held sway, but just as all dissenting preachers were not patriots, so all Anglicans were not Tories. It took a Tory, Peter Oliver, to pay the ultimate (if hostile) compliment to the political and intellectual importance of those members of the American clergy who spoke out in the American cause:

> As to their Pulpits, many of them were converted into Gutters of Sedition, the Torrents bore down all before them. The Clergy had quite unlearned the Gospel, & had substituted Politicks in its Stead.

The political thinkers of the Revolution found their way to contemporary and future audiences through every possible outlet. The agencies of communication of the past, like those of the present, were co-operative instruments of public opinion. An important piece of political thought that appeared in one of these agencies was certain to be copied or mentioned almost immediately in three or four others. Yet each of these channels did have its own special audience:

The Pamphlet. The most effective weapon of political argument was the pamphlet. In our search for the dominant principles of the Revolution, we must turn first to the hundreds of examples of this near-forgotten art. Otis's *Rights of the British Colonies,* John Adams's *Thoughts on Government,* Hamilton's *The Farmer Refuted,* Bland's *Inquiry into the Rights of the British Colonies,* Jefferson's *Summary View,* and Paine's best-selling *Common Sense* were perhaps the most influential instances of the use of this technique. Almost all important colonial pamphlets were reprinted immediately in London, where they were greeted by a flood of opposing pamphlets.

The Newspaper Article. Several key figures of the Revolution favored the press as an arena in which to argue, principally because a well-written article or letter in a local weekly was certain to be reprinted in other Whig newspapers throughout the colonies. Dickinson's "Letters from a Farmer in Pennsylvania," which appeared first in the *Pennsylvania Chronicle* in 1767-1768 and was reprinted in full in all but three or four journals in the colonies, is the most famous instance of political writing for the press. John Adams's "Dissertation on the Canon and Feudal Law" and "Novanglus," Arthur Lee's "Monitor," and Samuel Adams's "Vindex" were other pieces that appeared first in the newspapers. Nor must we overlook the thousands of articles and letters whose unknown authors helped shape Revolutionary thought, articles signed Chronus, Rusticus, Junius, Cato, Verus, Sydney, Benevolus, Benevolentior, A Female American, A Whig, Ploughjogger, Yet a Free Citizen, Foresight, A

Friend to Liberty and Property, Americanus, Solomon, Solomon Junior, Nil Desperandum de Patria, or any one of hundreds of other names and slogans that spoke of English and Roman liberty. Even when we manage to identify crafty Sam Adams with twenty-five different pseudonyms in the *Boston Gazette* and *Massachusetts Spy*, we still can recognize in the pseudonymous articles and letters of the decade a groundswell of popular political thought. No one who has been through the files of the *Boston Gazette, Massachusetts Spy, New-York Journal, Newport Mercury,* and *Pennsylvania Journal*—or of such less celebrated weeklies as *Dunlap's Maryland Gazette* and the *Norwich Packet*—can fail to agree with a penman of the times that "the PRESS hath never done greater Service since its first Invention." Its service to political thought was as imposing as its service to political action. A Tory writer in the *Boston Evening-Post* in 1769 complained that the Whig press had made it possible for "the peasants and their housewives in every part of the land . . . to dispute on politics and positively to determine upon our liberties." Pro Rege et Grege, Be Angry and Sin Not, a Patagonian, and Ichabod Snuffle have a very special place among the makers of American intellectual history.

The Broadside. This channel of communication was used to call patriots to action rather than to discuss major issues with any show of depth or dispassion. Yet "The Alarm," a series of broadsides published in New York over the pseudonym Hampden during the tea crisis in 1773, presented one of the best short treatises on property and the unalienable character of natural rights to appear in the Revolutionary period. Even in these ephemeral throwaways, so often satirical, demogogic, or downright abusive, we find useful examples of the recurrence to first principles.

The Almanac. The almanac, which had built up a mass audience in the first half of the eighteenth century, remained as popular as ever in the years of struggle with England. The printer of the almanac, who was anxious to preserve his special slice of that audience by giving it what it wanted, followed the trend of the times by offering poems, essays, couplets, and slogans about liberty, taxation, and John Locke. The almanacs of Nathaniel Ames are an especially rich storehouse of common political notions.

The Sermon. The "thundering pulpit," which through at least half the colonial period had been the only significant agency of communication, continued to reach tens of thousands who had no time or urge to read pamphlets and newspapers. While Mayhew, Chauncy, Cooke, and Cooper worked their chief influence in print, the forgotten ministers of hundreds of country churches proved once again the power of the spoken word. Requested by the Provincial Congress to "make the question of the rights of the colonies . . . a topic of the pulpit on week days," the Massachusetts clergy responded by making it the topic on Sundays as well. The principles of the Revolution had their broadest appeal in New England towns, and the eloquence of the clergy was more instrumental than the writings of Otis and the Adamses in bringing this about. At the same time, the printed sermon competed with the political pamphlet and newspaper article for first place in patriot affections. The annual election sermon in Connecticut and Massachusetts took on new meaning in these years of crisis. The election sermons of 1770—preached by Samuel

Cooke in Massachusetts and Stephen Johnson in Connecticut—were among the best tracts in political thought in the whole Revolutionary era.

The Oration. The spoken and printed sermon had its lay counterpart in the oration, a formal address devoted to advancing the patriot cause. Commencement pieces of students at Harvard and the Philadelphia Academy are one fruitful source of contemporary political ideas; speeches of Sons of Liberty at the dedication of their famous poles and trees are another. The annual oration on March 5 in Boston, a patriot device designed to keep alive the memory of the Massacre, was designed, in the words of one of its sponsors, "to preserve in the Minds of the People a lively Sense of the Danger of standing Armies." The student of Revolutionary attitudes toward civil and military power finds exactly what he is looking for in the March 5 orations of James Lovell, John Hancock, Joseph Warren, and Benjamin Church.

The Letter. In any study of an age in which few men had leisure or talent for formal political speculation, public and private letters of leading men of action are especially valuable as sources of political ideas. Public letters, those written designedly for publication, were a standard part of early journalism. Many private letters were also influential as agencies of communication, passed as they were from hand to hand among patriot leaders. The letters of men like the Adamses, the Lees, James Iredell, and Franklin—whether public, private, or secret—are a welcome addition to their more formal writings.

The Official Paper. Petitions to King and Parliament, public letters to members of the English ministry, resolutions, remonstrances, statements of grievances, declarations of rights, instructions to representatives, exchanges with royal governors, charges to grand juries, and grand jury presentments—in these and other official papers the colonists agitated the ideas of the Revolution. The interdependence of the agencies of communication is evident in the fact that Samuel Adams, Dickinson, and Jefferson based official documents on their own previous writings, and that patriot publishers hurried the results into print in pamphlets and newspapers. A set of resolutions on the Stamp Act adopted by the town meeting of Little Compton, Rhode Island, or a charge to the grand jury delivered by a patriot judge like Drayton might find its way into a dozen newspapers throughout the colonies. An appeal of Congress to the people of England or Quebec was certain to be picked up by the London press.

Although many official papers were worded to fit the occasion or audience and were thus not always honestly expressive of the sentiments of their authors, they light up the common ground on which patriots of differing views could meet in harmony. The address of Congress to "the Inhabitants of the Province of Quebec" of October 26, 1774, offers a unique catalogue of those political and social rights which colonists held closest to their hearts. Drayton's charge to the grand jury in Charleston May 2, 1776, is one of the most illuminating statements of the period about the right of the people to resist a tyrant king. The *Essex Result,* a commentary on the proposed Massachusetts Constitution of 1778 written by Theophilus Parsons for a convention at Ipswich, is one of the three or four most profound pieces of general speculation in the entire Revolutionary period. Town meetings, county courts, assemblies, and Continental Congresses were all contributors to American political thought. The memorable fact about their papers is not so much that Samuel Adams or Jefferson or Bland wrote them, but that official bodies were willing to express as their collective sentiments the political philosophies these penmen had worked out in their studies. The official paper reached its zenith in the Declaration of Independence, the Virginia Declaration of Rights, and the best of the early state constitutions, all eminent expressions of the political thought of the Revolution.

The one type of writing missing from this outpouring of political literature was the lengthy, careful, speculative treatise. No Hobbes or Rousseau or Locke arose in America to pronounce in one glorious book a political theory worthy of an age of revolution and constitution-making. Americans would wait another ten years after 1776 even to read such treatises as *The Federalist* and John Adams's *Defence of the Constitutions*. In the meantime, they strove to make up in volume and popularity for what their thinking lacked in depth and originality. It often seems that all America had taken to heart John Adams's exhortation of 1765:

Let us tenderly and kindly cherish, therefore, the means of knowledge. Let us dare to read, think, speak, and write. Let every order and degree among the people rouse their attention and animate their resolution. . . .

Let the pulpit resound with the doctrines and sentiments of religious liberty. . . . Let us see delineated before us the true map of man. Let us hear the dignity of his nature, and the noble rank he holds among the works of God,—that consenting to slavery is a sacrilegious breach of trust, as offensive in the sight of God as it is derogatory from our own honor or interest or happiness,—and that God Almighty has promulgated from heaven, liberty, peace, and good-will to man!

Let the bar proclaim, "the laws, the rights, the generous plan of power," delivered down from remote antiquity,—inform the world of the mighty struggles and numberless sacrifices made by our ancestors in defence of freedom. Let it be known, that British liberties are not the grants of princes or parliaments, but original rights, conditions of original contracts, coequal with prerogative, and coeval with government; that many of our rights are inherent and essential, agreed on as maxims, and established as preliminaries, even before a parliament existed. Let them search for the foundations of British laws and government in the frame of human nature, in the constitution of the intellectual and moral world. . . .

Let the colleges join their harmony in the same delightful concert. Let every declamation turn upon the beauty of liberty and virtue, and the deformity, turpitude, and malignity, of slavery and vice. Let the public disputations become researches into the grounds and nature and ends of government, and the means of preserving the good and demolishing the evil. Let the dialogues, and all the exercises, become the instruments of impressing on this tender mind, and of spreading and distributing far and wide, the ideas of right and the sensations of freedom.

In a word, let every sluice of knowledge be opened and set a-flowing.

And so, indeed, was every sluice of knowledge "set a-flowing," much to the indignation of the British ministry and the instruction of the world.

TWO

The Problem of
the American Spokesmen

AMERICAN LEADERS had two ends in view as they ma-
neuvered their way through the confusing decade that
led to Philadelphia and 1776: one immediate, to resist
and seek repeal of each oppressive act of Parliament or
related policy of the ministry; and one long-range, to find
the proper place for the colonies within the protecting
pale of the rising British Empire. In the first instance, the
prime constitutional issue was the power of Parliament
to tax the colonies; in the second, and ultimately more
important and perplexing, it was the power of Crown
and Parliament together to govern them, whether by
taxation, legislation, supervision, inspection, royal veto,
or other means. The chief constitutional problem was
therefore to find the line, if such there was, between the
general authority of Parliament and special authority of
each colonial assembly, between total submission and
independence. We cannot investigate the political
thought of the Revolution unless we first recall this great
problem in constitutional law, the organization of the

British Empire, for at every stage of the imperial controversy the Americans appealed to first principles in support of their current constitutional stand. Political thought justified the first show of resistance; political thought was the final answer to the constitutional problem. Government by consent and the rights of man were the only theoretical foundation upon which independence could in the end be based.

It is impossible to fix precisely the state of American opinion at any given time concerning the confused relationship between England and the colonies. Men who shared the same political views found themselves in clear if amiable disagreement over the central constitutional issue. Some shifted their opinions from one crisis to the next, driving a Virginian to protest in 1774: "Shall we, Proteus-like, perpetually change our ground, assume every moment some new and strange shape, to defend, to evade?" Others, notably James Otis and Richard Bland, expressed two or three different interpretations in one pamphlet. Few Americans voiced their opinions in words that meant the same thing to all men. The problem of locating the line was a formidable one, principally because few men had ever tried to locate it before except in terms of subjection or independence. The result was a discouraging confusion of language and opinion. The most we can say is that all patriots began with a hazy belief in home rule quite opposed to the assumptions of the Stamp and Declaratory Acts, and moved at different speeds in the direction of a dominion theory of the British Empire. At least seven different solutions to the problem of imperial organization were brought forward at one time or another during this period.

Complete Subjection and Virtual Representation. The doctrine of the Declaratory Act of 1766—that the King in Parliament had "full power and authority to make laws and statutes of sufficient force and validity to bind the colonies and people of *America*, subjects of the Crown of *Great Britain*, in all cases whatsoever"—was apparently acceptable to only one leader of American thought, James Otis, and even he was not entirely convinced

that the Parliament of Great-Britain hath a just, clear, equitable and constitutional right, power and authority, to bind the colonies, by all acts wherein they are named.

Nowhere else in patriot literature, certainly after 1765, was the Tory dogma of complete subjection treated with any attitude but contempt.

The chief historical interest of this dogma lies in the corollary through which ministerial supporters tried to make it palatable to colonial tastes: virtual representation. This argument was designed to silence the cry of "no taxation without representation" by reviving and extending the ancient fiction that all Englishmen, whether enfranchised or not, were represented "virtually" in Parliament. The colonies, asserted Tory writers, stood in the same constitutional and practical position as the cities of Manchester and Sheffield. That they elected no representatives did not mean they were unrepresented and therefore taxed without their consent, for each member of the House of Commons, whether from London or Old Sarum, represented the interests of all Englishmen. In the weighty words of none other than Dr. Samuel Johnson:

Our nation is represented in parliament by an assembly as numerous as can well consist with order and dispatch, chosen by persons so differently qualified in different places, that the mode of choice seems to be, for the most part, formed by chance, and settled by custom. Of individuals far the greater part have no vote, and of the voters few have any personal knowledge of him to whom they intrust their liberty and fortune.

Yet this representation has the whole effect expected or desired; that of spreading so wide the care of general interest, and the participation of publick counsels, that the advantage or corruption of particular men can seldom operate with much injury to the Publick.

For this reason many populous and opulent towns neither enjoy nor desire particular representatives; they are included in the general scheme of public administration, and cannot suffer but with the rest of the empire.

The American answer to virtual representation was a mixture of irritation and contempt. "Our *privileges* are all *virtual*," Arthur Lee shouted, "our sufferings are *real*." Most writers rejected in just such a sentence or paragraph the sophistry of virtual representation, refusing to dignify it with lengthy rebuttal. James Otis spoke the colonial mind when he rattled off his famous retort:

To what purpose is it to ring everlasting changes to the colonists on the cases of Manchester, Birmingham and Sheffield, who return no members? If those now so considerable places are not represented, they ought to be. . . . It may perhaps sound strangely to some, but it is in my most humble opinion as good *law* and as good *sense* too, to affirm that all the plebeians of Great-Britain are in fact or virtually represented in the assembly of the Tuskarora's, as that all the colonists are in fact or virtually represented in the honourable house of Commons of Great-Britain.

A few colonists took the doctrine of virtual representation seriously enough to refute it with a careful show of history and logic. The most convincing objector was Daniel Dulany, jr., of Maryland, later to become a loyalist, who devoted some of the best pages of a pamphlet on taxation to demolishing virtual representation. This doctrine, he asserted in his *Considerations on the Propriety of Imposing Taxes in the British Colonies,* "consists of Facts not true and of Conclusions inadmissible," and "is a mere Cob-web, spread to catch the unwary, and entangle the weak." The key paragraph of his argument was this:

There is not that intimate and inseparable Relation between the *Electors of Great-Britain* and the *Inhabitants of the Colonies,* which must inevitably involve both in the same Taxation; on the contrary, not a single *actual* Elector in *England,* might be immediately affected by a Taxation in *America,* imposed by a Statute which would have a general Operation and Effect, upon the Properties of the Inhabitants of the Colonies. The latter might be oppressed in a Thousand Shapes, without any Sympathy, or exciting any Alarm in the former. Moreover, even Acts, oppressive and injurious to the Colonies in an extreme Degree, might become popular in *England,* from the Promise of Expectation that the very Measures which depressed the Colonies, would give Ease to the Inhabitants of *Great-Britain.*

Richard Bland, Maurice Moore of North Carolina, Edward Bancroft, John Dickinson, and Arthur Lee were other dissenters from this doctrine.

Representation in Parliament. One small band of patriots, for whom Otis and Franklin were spokesmen, proposed that the colonies be "represented in some proportion to their number and estates, in the grand legislature of the nation." In his *Rights of the British Colonies* Otis wrote:

A representation in Parliament from the several Colonies, since they are become so large and numerous, as to be called on not to maintain provincial government, civil and military among themselves, for this they have chearfully done, but to contribute towards the support of a national standing army, by reason of the heavy national debt . . . can't be tho't an unreasonable thing, nor if asked, could it be called an immodest request. . . . Besides the equity of an American representation in parliament, a thousand advantages would result from it. It would be the most effectual means of giving those of both countries a thorough knowledge of each others interests; as well as that of the whole, which are inseparable.

Neither Otis nor Franklin advanced this solution with any real show of conviction, for it proved equally distasteful to leaders and led on both sides of the ocean. The equity of American representation was not admitted by Parliament, the advantages were not at all clear to the colonists. The arguments of the Adamses were representative of an overwhelming colonial opinion. Samuel Adams wrote to the colony's agent in 1765:

We are far however from desiring any Representation there, because we think the Colonies cannot be equally and fully represented; and if not equally then in Effect not at all. A Representative should be, and continue to be well acquainted with the internal Circumstances of the People whom he represents. . . . Now the Colonies are at so great a Distance from the Place where the Parliament meets, from which they are separated by a wide Ocean; and their Circumstances are so often and continually varying, as is the Case in all Countries not fully settled, that it would not be possible for Men, tho' ever so well acquainted with them at the Beginning of a Parliament, to continue to have an adequate Knowledge of them during the Existence of that Parliament.

And John Adams queried his readers in 1775:

Would not representatives in the house of commons, unless they were numerous in proportion to the numbers of people in America, be a snare rather than a blessing?

Would Britain ever agree to a proportionable number of American members; and if she would, could America support the expense of them?

Could American representatives possibly know the sense, the exigencies, &c. of their constituents, at such a distance, so perfectly as it is absolutely necessary legislators should know?

Could Americans ever come to the knowledge of the behavior of their members, so as to dismiss the unworthy?

Would Americans in general ever submit to septennial elections?

Have we not sufficient evidence, in the general frailty and depravity of human nature . . . that a deep, treacherous, plausible, corrupt minister would be able to seduce our members to betray us as fast as we could send them?

Imperial federation was unacceptable to colonial minds on historical, psychological, and practical grounds. To send a few representatives to England would serve only to legalize taxation by Parliament, not prevent it.

Internal and External Taxation. The threat and passage of the Stamp Act evoked the first unsuccessful attempt to locate a fixed line between parliamentary and provincial power: the distinction between excise taxes (internal taxation) and custom duties (external taxation). Although recent researches have demonstrated that this formula was neither so clear-cut nor popular as his-

torians have hitherto assumed, many Americans did subscribe to the general notion that Parliament had the right
to pass the Sugar Act of 1764 but not the Stamp Act of
1765. The protests and pamphlets of 1765-1766 did not
express this distinction so clearly as they might have,
principally because the colonists saw no reason to approve
a bad act in order to destroy an evil one. They talked a
great deal about internal taxation, since that is what they
were denying. They talked very little about external taxation, since to approve it positively was not essential to
their arguments and to deny it flatly was not yet essential
to their liberties. Therefore, while they resisted the Stamp
Act, attacking it on grounds of unconstitutionality, they
acquiesced in the Sugar Act, attacking it on grounds of
inexpediency.

In point of fact, the distinction was quite untenable,
and many leading Americans shunned it from the beginning. Otis, the lone wolf who argued against British
policies while conceding their constitutionality, asserted
flatly that "there is no foundation for the distinction
some make in England, between an internal and an external tax on the colonies," and added "that the Parliament of Great-Britain has a just and equitable right,
power and authority, to *impose taxes on the colonies,
internal and external, on lands, as well as on trade.*" But
English friends of America found this formula so useful
that they converted it into a working principle of the
imperial constitution. Enough had been said about "internal taxes" in official resolutions and in pamphlets like
Dulany's *Considerations*, Bland's *Inquiry*, and Stephen
Hopkins's *Grievances of the American Colonies* to convince Pitt—and indeed Franklin—that the colonists had
adopted the distinction as their own key to the imperial

relationship. The implications of Dulany's widely read argument, which did not even use the phrase "external taxes," were good enough for Pitt. Having cut through Dulany's confusion to an interpretation that suited his own ends, he could blow down an obstreperous but also more perceptive member with the annoyed remark, "If the gentleman does not understand the difference between internal and external taxes, I cannot help it." Whether American or English in origin, the distinction was unworkable, as Charles Townshend was able to demonstrate in 1767 with his program of import duties on lead, glass, paint, paper, and tea.

Taxation for Revenue and Taxation for Regulation of Trade. In the course of an examination before the House of Commons February 13, 1766, Franklin was asked if his countrymen had given much thought to the supposed distinction between internal and external taxation. "They never have hitherto," he answered, adding:

Many arguments have been used here to shew them, that there is no difference, and that, if you have no right to tax them internally, you have none to tax them externally, or make any other law to bind them. At present they do not reason so; but in time they may possibly be convinced by these arguments.

Franklin, at least the public Franklin, was behind the onward surge of American opinion. Many colonists were already convinced that there was no distinction between these two forms of taxation. The Townshend duties of 1767, which were based squarely on the distinction, forced them now to deny it positively.

Townshend's error, of course, had been to announce in the legislation itself that the revenues from these duties would be used for a specific and highly unpopular purpose, that of "defraying the charge of the administration of justice, and the support of the civil government in such provinces where it shall be found necessary." Many Americans now raised a new distinction, already implicit in numerous resolves and pamphlets, between taxation for revenue (unconstitutional) and taxation as part of a scheme for regulating imperial trade (constitutional). The area of unconstitutionality was expanded to include not only all internal taxes but those external taxes which were designed to produce revenue. The chief spokesman for this solution was John Dickinson. In his fantastically popular "Letters from a Farmer in Pennsylvania" he stated the new doctrine in these words:

The parliament unquestionably possesses a legal authority to *regulate* the trade of *Great-Britain*, and all her colonies. Such an authority is essential to the relation between a mother country and her colonies; and necessary for the common good of all. . . .

I have looked over *every statute* relating to these colonies, from their settlement to this time; and I find every one of them founded on this principle, till the *Stamp-Act* administration. *All before,* are calculated to regulate trade, and preserve or promote a mutually beneficial intercourse between the several constituent parts of the empire; and though many of them imposed duties on trade, yet those duties were always imposed *with design* to restrain the commerce of one part, that was injurious to another, and thus to promote the general welfare. The raising a revenue thereby was never intended. Thus the King, by his judges in his courts of justice, imposes fines which all together amount to a very considerable sum, and contribute to the support of government: But this is merely a consequence arising from restrictions, that only meant to keep peace, and prevent confusion; and surely a man would argue very loosely, who should conclude from hence, that the King has a right to levy money in general upon his subjects. Never did the *British* parliament, till the period above mentioned, think of imposing duties in *America*, FOR THE PURPOSE OF RAISING A REVENUE. . . .

Here [in the Townshend Acts] we may observe an authority *expressly* claimed and exerted to impose duties on these colonies; not for the regulation of trade; not for the preservation or promotion of a mutually beneficial intercourse between the several constituent parts of the empire, heretofore the *sole objects* of parliamentary institutions; *but for the single purpose of levying money upon us.*

This I call an innovation; and a most dangerous innovation.

The difficulty with this distinction, as critics on both sides of the ocean were quick to point out, could be framed in the simple question: What if a trade regulation should produce revenue? To this Dickinson answered:

The *nature* of any impositions laid by parliament on these colonies, must determine the *design* in laying them. It may not be easy in every instance to discover that design. Wherever it is doubtful, I think submission cannot be dangerous; nay, it must be right; for in my opinion, there is no privilege these colonies claim, which they ought in *duty* and *prudence* more earnestly to maintain and defend, than the authority of the *British* parliament to regulate the trade of all her dominions.

The criterion of intent satisfied no one for long. Radical colonists were anxious to erect a constitutional barrier that left a good deal less scope to parliamentary discretion. Defenders of the English point of view asserted that it was "only a pretense under which to strip Parliament of all jurisdiction over the colonies." Dickinson's legalistic attempt to give precision to a vague boundary was doomed to failure. Yet until 1775 patriot writers made use of the distinction between "taxation" for revenue and "impositions" for regulation of trade.

Denial of Taxation; Home Rule. The next step beyond Dickinson, to which less cautious men had already pushed, was a doctrine of home rule that denied taxation of any description and admitted legislation only for concerns clearly imperial in nature. Clear-sighted men in both camps had already pointed to the absurdity of considering internal taxation and internal legislation as two different things, realizing that laws could do more than taxes to correct or impair the situation created by the long years of "salutary neglect." Several tough-minded legislatures had seized upon the Stamp Act to voice constitutional objections to parliamentary legislation "respecting their internal Polity," and some movers of these resolutions had gone on to expand upon this point in the first searching pamphlets. This, for example, was the general if confused position taken by Richard Bland in his *Inquiry* of 1766. It was a position implicit in many later resolutions and pamphlets, especially after such shows of force as the act of 1767 suspending the New York Assembly; it was the position finally adopted by conservative patriots like John Dickinson. His *Essay on the Constitutional Power,* published in July, 1774, was the best and final statement of the doctrine of home rule, of exemption from Parliament's power to tax at all and to legislate on matters not clearly imperial in scope.

A Dominion Theory of the British Empire. By 1773 Governor Hutchinson of Massachusetts had lost both his good will and perspective. "I know of no line," he wrote to the Massachusetts legislature, "that can be drawn between the supreme authority of Parliament and the total independence of the colonies: it is impossible there should be two independent Legislatures in one and the same state." "If there be no such line," answered the lower house, with the help of John Adams, "the consequence is, either that the colonies are the vassals of the Parliament, or that they are totally independent." But there was yet a third possibility: the union of the colonies and England "in one head and common Sovereign." Thus, under pressure of events at home and abroad, the colonists arrived at a final theory of imperial organization that was still one step short of independence.

This dominion theory of the empire, which held simply and prophetically that the only constitutional tie between the colonies and England was a common sovereign, had been long in the making. As early as 1765 men were reaching out for this radical solution, and in 1768 Franklin could reflect:

The more I have thought and read on the subject, the more I find myself confirmed in opinion, that no middle doctrine can be well maintained, I mean not clearly with intelligible arguments. Something might be made of either of the extremes; that Parliament has a power to make *all laws* for us, or that it has a power to make *no laws* for us; and I think the arguments for the latter more numerous and weighty, than those for the former. Supposing that doctrine established, the colonies would then be so many separate states, only subject to the same king, as England and Scotland were before the union.

By 1770 Franklin was no longer in doubt, nor, for that matter, were several other leaders of the American cause. Not until 1774, however, was the dominion theory put forward without apologies or qualifications. John Adams's "Novanglus," Jefferson's *Summary View*, Hamilton's *The Farmer Refuted*, and James Iredell's "To the Inhabitants of Great Britain" all arrived simultaneously at these conclusions: that the power of Parliament to lay taxes or pass laws for the colonies was "none at all"; that the colonies had voluntarily, by "free, cheerful consent," allowed Parliament the "power of regulating trade"; and that the "fealty and allegiance of Americans" was due only "to the person of King George III, whom God long preserve and prosper." The most brilliant statement of this position was James Wilson's *Considerations on the Nature and Extent of the Legislative Authority of the British Parliament*. The future justice of the Supreme Court of an independent America rested the case for equality of states in the British Empire not only on law and history, but on "natural right," "the principles of liberty," and "the happiness of the colonies" as well. Wilson's opening passage tells us graphically of the pains with which men like Wilson, Franklin, and John Adams groped in good faith for a line between parliamentary and provincial power:

The following sheets were written during the late non-importation agreement: but that agreement being dissolved before they were ready for the press, it was then judged unseasonable to publish them. Many will, perhaps, be surprised to see the legislative authority of the British parliament over the colonies denied *in every instance*. Those the writer informs, that, when he began this piece, he would probably have been surprised at such an opinion himself; for that it was the *result*, and not the *occasion*, of his disquisitions. He entered upon them with a view and expectation of being able to trace some constitutional line between those cases in which we ought, and those in which we ought not, to acknowledge the power of parliament over us. In the prosecution of his inquiries, he became fully convinced that such a line does not exist; and that there can be no medium between acknowledging and denying that power in *all* cases. Which of these two alternatives is most consistent with law, with the principles of liberty, and with the happiness of the colonies, let the publick determine.

The closing paragraphs of Wilson's *Considerations* mark the abandonment of the attempt to admit Parliament to some sort of authority over the colonies. It was now considered "repugnant to the essential maxims of jurisprudence, to the ultimate end of all governments, to the genius of the British constitution, and to the liberty and happiness of the colonies, that they should be bound by the legislative authority of the parliament of Great Britain."

There is another, and a much more reasonable meaning, which may be intended by the dependence of the colonies on Great Britain. The phrase may be used to denote the obedience and loyalty, which the colonists owe to the *kings* of Great Britain. . . .

Those who launched into the unknown deep, in quest of new countries and habitations, still considered themselves as subjects of the English monarchs, and behaved suitably to that character; but it no where appears, that they still considered themselves as represented in an English parliament, or that they thought the authority of the English parliament extended over them. . . .

This is a dependence, which they have acknowledged hitherto; which they acknowledge now; and which, if it is reasonable to judge of the future by the past and the present, they will continue to acknowledge hereafter. . . .

From this dependence . . . arises a strict connexion between the inhabitants of Great Britain and those of America. They are fellow subjects; they are under allegiance to the same prince; and this union of allegiance naturally produces a union of hearts. It is also productive of a union of measures through the whole British dominions. To the king is intrusted the direction and management of the great machine of government. . . .

The connexion and harmony between Great Britain and us, which it is her interest and ours mutually to cultivate, and on which her prosperity, as well as ours, so materially depends, will be better preserved by the operation of the legal prerogatives of the crown, than by the exertion of an unlimited authority by parliament.

Even in this apparently clear-cut solution American spokesmen stood on confused ground, for in their anxiety to exclude Parliament from their affairs they had come dangerously near to a wholesale revival of the royal prerogative. Had this solution actually been given a trial, could they conceivably have been satisfied? The next step had to be independence.

Independence. From the dominion status of 1774 to independence in 1776 was an easy road in political and constitutional theory. If history and natural law justified immunity from the authority of Parliament, so, too, did they justify deposing a wicked King. Up to 1774 Americans had done little thinking in this vein. The authority of Parliament had been the bone of contention, and the participation of the King in the exercise of that authority had been studiously or carelessly ignored. The only independence the colonists sought was independence of Parliament. The publication of Jefferson's *Summary View* in 1774 gave a brand-new twist to the imperial tie. At the same time that it reduced the imperial problem to a simple question of personal allegiance to a common sovereign, it made clear that colonists were learning to distinguish the actions of the sovereign from those of Parliament. The Virginia radical made separate listings of Parliament's usurpations and George III's "deviations from the line of duty," and warned the King that persistence in these deviations could lead to a severing of the last bond of empire.

The final stage of American argument is, of course, most plainly read in the Declaration of Independence, in which the dominion theory and natural law were skillfully woven together to justify the bold decision to dissolve an empire. Thanks to the dominion theory of 1774, the Americans could ignore Parliament almost completely and concentrate their fire on George III. Having already proved, largely through their own reading of history, that they were totally outside the jurisdiction of Parliament and were subjects of the King by free choice, they had only to prove to a candid world that the latter, not the former, had played the tyrant. And it was exactly here, at the moment when they renounced a covenanted monarch, that the whole theory of natural law proved its worth to a people who prided themselves on their political morality. This theory had been extremely helpful at every stage of the struggle since 1765. In this final stage it was absolutely essential.

THREE

The Characteristics of Political Writing

POLITICAL WRITING in the years of the American Revolution was shaped by circumstances of time, place, purpose, and tradition. The kind of political commentary in which colonial authors indulged was an intriguing blend of old English and new American attitudes, beliefs, and prejudices. We must understand clearly the major characteristics of public disputation in this golden age of American political thought.

Occasionalism. Much serious political writing in this period was occasional, even opportunistic in nature. The pamphlets, speeches, resolutions, and sermons supporting the American cause were the work of busy men with little time or appetite for long, hard thoughts, of men who, through no fault of their own, could no more seize the initiative in print than they could in action. Each political writing, like each political maneuver, was largely a reaction to English policy and argument. The ministry planned, Parliament legislated, and word of a new policy reached America; as if in conditioned response, pamphlets and resolutions poured from the presses, all bearing the stamp of the occasional performance. Few writers, however, were as honest as Rev. John Allen, who ended his *Beauties of Liberty* with the apology, "This Peice comes into the World, as Men go through it, with many faults." The total impression one gets from the vast literature of the period is indeed one of many faults—of haste, superficiality, repetition, and ambiguity. Hardly a single example of political, economic, or constitutional argument was the work of a man who had approached his writing desk with deliberate tread. Wilson's *Considerations* and John Adams's *Dissertation* were two of the few exceptions to this broad statement. A writer disguised as The Centinel was all too correct when he told his countrymen in a letter to the *Massachusetts Spy*:

There is scarce a man in the community, but what will tell you he is an Englishman, a freeman, and that he glories in the nature of that government under which he lives. But ask him what he means by being a freeman, desire him to explain to you the properties, and the eminently glorious principles which are contained in this constitution, and you nonplus him and find very few satisfactory answers to the enquiry. The bulk of the citizens, as they enjoy the happiness resulting herefrom, seldom take pains to examine the constituent principles, as perhaps business, avocations, and many other causes render it impracticable.

A consequence of this occasionalism was the extravagant confusion that marred the discussion of imperial organization. Bland and Otis were surely not so confused in mind as they were in print, but consistency was apparently worth sacrificing to a printer's deadline. Another example was the indiscriminate appeal to any and every type of higher law against oppressive acts of Parliament: charters, common law, Magna Charta, the British Constitution, and "the law of God and nature." But would it have aided the American cause had the colonists decided which of these defenses—"the immutable laws of nature, the principles of the English constitution, and the several charters or compacts"—they proposed to rely upon most heavily? At least some of the confusion in colonial arguments must have been calculated to confuse.

Propaganda. Few American writers were entirely honest in method. Hyperbole, misrepresentation, and the appeal to fear were overworked techniques. Black and white were the shades most used in argument. The equation of the small evil with the big was a particular favorite. Any show of ministerial determination was "arbitrary power." The slightest hint of obedience to the hated acts was "compleat slavery" or "Egyptian bondage." George III was either the "best of Kings" or the "Royal Brute." It is not in disparagement of America pamphleteers, who wrote to win a great cause rather than the approval of critics yet unborn, to say that they rank with liberty's most effective political propagandists.

Political argument reached heights of make-believe in the outcry against "Popery" and the "Papists." Fear of Catholicism was strong throughout the colonies, and no small service was rendered the American cause by authors who gave their audience no choice except "Liberty and Protestantism" and "Popery and arbitrary Power." No doubt many colonists were profoundly concerned about the future of dissenting Protestantism under English rule, but they were hardly so many or so concerned as to justify the thousands of pages devoted to this issue. It must often have seemed to the newspaper reader of the day that the real goal of the British ministry was to extend Roman Catholicism rather than imperial control. The clamor about "Popery," in which many writers who should have known better joined with a will, was most deafening in 1768-1769, at the time of the agitation over an American episcopate, and in 1774, after the passage of the Quebec Act. Samuel Adams, the master propagandist, recognized the usefulness of this issue by penning a series of articles to the *Boston Gazette* in which he made statements about English designs that even he could not have believed for a moment.

The Anson County Committee of Safety down in North Carolina thought it had pushed the Catholic argument as far as it would go when it told a certain doubter in 1774 that

Lord North was a Roman Catholick, that the King's crown tottered upon his shoulders, for he had established the Roman Catholick Religion in the Province of Quebec, and that the King and Parliament did intend to establish Popery on all the Continent of America.

But a Philadelphia patriot had already outdone them in a piece in the *Pennsylvania Packet* that reached this climax:

We may live to see our churches converted into mass houses, and lands plundered of tythes for the support of a Popish clergy. The Inquisition may erect her standard in Pennsylvania and the city of Philadelphia may yet experience the carnage of a St. Bartholomew's day.

The loose or designed use of "Communism" today has an exact counterpart in the use of "Popery" in the Revolutionary crisis. The way, for example, to dispose of

General Gage was to brand him "a Papist in politicks." What could have been easier, or more full of guile?

The catalogue of grievances against Crown or Parliament was another technique used to full advantage. The Declaration of Independence was the best known of these statements which combined truth and hyperbole in amounts calculated to convince the irresolute of the evil designs of the mother country. This effective indictment of George III was, like the Revolution itself, the work of a determined minority that could hardly have afforded to be more straightforward and moderate in statement. Propaganda was a faithful servant of liberty in this decisive decade.

Legalism. In his speech on conciliation with the colonies, March 22, 1775, Edmund Burke spoke in evident admiration of a feature of American politics and political discussion. The fifth item in his list of the "variety of powerful causes" giving rise to the "fierce spirit of liberty . . . in the English Colonies" was education in the law:

Permit me, sir, to add another circumstance in our colonies, which contributes no mean part towards the growth and effect of this untractable spirit. I mean their education. In no country perhaps in the world is the law so general a study. The profession itself is numerous and powerful; and in most provinces it takes the lead. The greater number of the deputies sent to the congress were lawyers. But all who read, and most do read, endeavor to obtain some smattering in that science. I have been told by an eminent bookseller, that in no branch of his business, after tracts of popular devotion, were so many books as those on the law exported to the plantations. The colonists have now fallen into the way of printing them for their own use. I hear that they have sold nearly as many

of Blackstone's Commentaries in America as in England. . . .
This study renders men acute, inquisitive, dexterous, prompt
in attack, ready in defence, full of resources. In other countries, the people, more simple, and of a less mercurial cast,
judge of an ill principle in government only by an actual
grievance; here they anticipate the evil, and judge of the
pressure of the grievance by the badness of the principle.
They augur misgovernment at a distance; and snuff the approach of tyranny in every tainted breeze.

The Revolutionary crisis marked the climax of an
historic process that had been generations in the making:
the seizure of political power by the legal profession. Otis,
Wilson, Dickinson, John Adams, Dulany, Jefferson,
Henry, Drayton, Iredell and dozens of other American
leaders were practicing lawyers; their assaults on English
policy were therefore thoroughly legalistic in approach
and expression. The argument from legal history—heavily
laden with citations to Bracton, Coke, Blackstone, Hale,
Holt, and other giants of English law—was a favorite
not only with these sons of the common law, but also,
as Burke pointed out, with those patriots who had only
a "smattering in that science." While Dickinson's "Letters" and Wilson's *Considerations* were the most refined
example of the lawyer's brief, hundreds of other pamphlets and letters exploited the widespread popularity
of this type of argument. Small wonder Tories were so
angry at the lawyers for "cultivating, with unwearied
Pains, the Seeds of Infatuation and Tumult." It must
often have seemed to the ministers of George III that
they were dealing with a race of legal historians.

Facts. "Let Facts be submitted to a candid World,"
commanded the delegates at Philadelphia, July 4, 1776,
thereby ending eleven years of debate in which the sub-

mission of facts, not all of them exactly candid, had been a major intellectual support of the American cause. The English-American had always been a handy man with economic and historical facts, with the appeal to common sense about the present and to common agreement about the past. Now in his time of trial and transition to independence he tried to ward off the policy of "ministerial vengeance" by showing its unworkability as well as its unconstitutionality. When every argument against the Stamp Act had been recited ten thousand times or more, the hardheaded replies of Franklin in the House of Commons proved the most persuasive of all:

Q. Are not the Colonies, from their circumstances, very able to pay the stamp duty?

A. In my opinion there is not gold and silver enough in the Colonies to pay the stamp duty for one year. . . .

Q. Can any thing less than a military force carry the stamp act into execution?

A. I do not see how a military force can be applied to that purpose.

Q. Why may it not?

A. Suppose a military force sent into America, they will find nobody in arms; what are they then to do? They cannot force a man to take stamps who chuses to do without them. They will not find a rebellion; they may indeed make one.

Q. If the act is not repealed, what do you think will be the consequences?

A. A total loss of the respect and affection the people of America bear to this country, and of all the commerce that depends on that respect and affection.

Q. How can the commerce be affected?

A. You will find, that if the act is not repealed, they will take very little of your manufactures in a short time.

Q. Is it in their power to do without them?

A. I think they may very well do without them.

Q. Is it their interest not to take them?

A. The goods they take from Britain are either necessaries, mere conveniences, or superfluities. The first, as cloth, &c. with a little industry they can make at home; the second they can do without, till they are able to provide them among themselves; and the last, which are much the greatest part, they will strike off immediately. They are mere articles of fashion, purchased and consumed because the fashion in a respected country; but will now be detested and rejected. The people have already struck off, by general agreement, the use of all goods fashionable in mournings, and many thousand pounds worth are sent back as unsaleable.

The calm recital of the harmful consequences of English policy—especially when harmful to England itself—was a powerful weapon of colonial argument. A pamphlet like the anonymous *Essay on the Trade of the Northern Colonies* (1764)—cool, moderate, reasonable, and above all factual—was worth a dozen apostrophes to abstract justice or reviews of legal history in the attempt to sway American and English opinion.

The appeal to facts, the invitation to hardheaded consideration of economic results, proved most popular in the same months when the "appeal to heaven" reached a climax. Many colonists who were convinced that America was entitled by "reason and justice" to seek independence had also to be convinced that they would be as well if not better off commercially. Paine's recital of grievances, abuse of monarchy, and interpretation of the "voice of nature and reason" in *Common Sense* were crushing blows for independence, but the most crushing of all was his simple remark, "Our corn will fetch its price in any market in Europe." The advantages of free trade with the world were played up by many authors with special earnestness, for example, by a correspondent of the *Philadelphia Evening Post* in February, 1776:

> What will be the probable benefits of independence? A free and unlimited trade; a great accession of wealth, and a proportionable rise in the value of land; the establishment, gradual improvement and perfection of manufactures and science; a vast influx of foreigners, encouraged by the mildness of a free, equal, and tolerating government to leave their native countries, and settle in these Colonies; an astonishing encrease of our people from the present stock. . . . WE CANNOT PAY TOO GREAT A PRICE FOR LIBERTY, AND POSTERITY WILL THINK INDEPENDENCE A CHEAP PURCHASE AT EIGHTEEN MILLIONS.

Independence, wrote a canny Scot in Princeton to his native countrymen all over America, would prove "both honourable and profitable to this country." Throughout this decade profit and loss vied with honor and dishonor as major themes of colonial polemics.

Conservatism. Perhaps the most remarkable feature of the political literature of this decade was its essential conservatism—a word, more than incidentally, used throughout this book in a broad and objective sense. If the Americans were the most successful revolutionaries of all time, they were revolutionaries by chance rather than choice. Until the last few months before independence the steady purpose of their resistance was to restore an old order rather than to build a new one, to get back, as Arthur Lee put it, to "the good days of George the second. There was no junto, no backstairs business then; a Whig King and Whig minister, speaking to a Whig people." Or as another patriot wrote in the *New-York Journal* in 1775:

The British Parliament is violently usurping the powers of our colony governments, and rendering our legal Assemblies utterly useless; to prevent this, the necessity of our situation has obliged us to depart from the common forms, and to adopt measures which would be otherwise unjustifiable; but, in this departure, we have been influenced by an ardent desire to repel innovations destructive to all good government among us, and fatal to the foundations of law, liberty, and justice: We have declared, in the most explicit terms, that we wish for nothing more, than a restoration to our ancient condition.

The ingrained conservatism of even the most high-spirited sermons and pamphlets is evident in four major themes that were chanted without pause: the invocation of the first settlers, the appeal to the ancient charters, veneration of the British Constitution and British rights, and homage to the monarchy. There is no reason to believe that until the Coercive Acts of 1774 or even later the American writers were not sincere in their wish, which Samuel Adams expressed for them, to be "restored to their original standing." The ministry, not they, had changed the rules of the game. They stood fast in the great tradition, "Whigs in a Reign when Whiggism is out of Fashion."

Americans in 1776 like Americans today were fond of invoking the example of "Ancestors remarkable for their Zeal for true Religion & Liberty." "Let us read and recollect and impress upon our souls," wrote John Adams to the Boston public, the views and ends of our own more immediate forefathers, in exchanging their native country for a dreary, inhospitable wilderness. Let us examine into the nature of that power, and the cruelty of that oppression, which drove them from their homes. Recollect their amazing fortitude, their bitter sufferings,—the hunger, the nakedness, the cold, which they patiently endured,—the severe labors of clearing their grounds, building their houses, raising their provisions, amidst dangers from wild beasts and savage men, before they had time or money or materials for commerce. Recollect the civil and religious principles and hopes and expectations which constantly supported and carried them through all hardships with patience and resignation. Let us recollect it was liberty, the hope of liberty for themselves and us and ours, which conquered all discouragements, dangers, and trials.

"Look back, therefore," echoed Provost Smith of Philadelphia,

with reverence look back to the times of ancient virtue and renown. Look back to the mighty purposes which your fathers had in view, when they traversed a vast ocean, and planted this land. Recal to your minds their labours, their toils, their perseverance, and let their divine spirit animate you in all your actions.

The Pilgrim Fathers were whirling in their graves a full 165 years before the founding of the American Liberty League: In 1769 a society was formed to commemorate annually the landing at Plymouth, and a good part of every celebration was devoted to a comparison of odious present with glorious past. Stephen Hopkins developed this theme in an account of the first settlers of Providence:

Nothing but extreme Diligence, and matchless Perseverance, could possibly have carried them through this Undertaking; could have procured them the scanty Morsels which supported a Life of Want and of Innocence. Too much have we their Descendants departed from the Diligence, Fortitude, Frugality, and Innocence of these our Fathers.

For the most part, however, the colonists called upon their ancestors to inspire rather than to chastise. "The famous Tools of Power are holding up the picture of Want and Misery," Samuel Adams wrote from beleaguered Boston in 1774, "but in vain do they think to intimidate us; The Virtue of our Ancestors inspires— they were content with Clams & Muscles."

The appeal to the charter in defense of colonial rights, a usage popular even with residents of colonies without charters, was a second instance of the conservative orientation of the American mind. In law the charters were not much more sacred than medieval grants and were open to attack from Parliament, courts, and Crown. But in the eyes of the colonists, especially the men of New England, they were unassailable declarations of "the rights and privileges of natural freeborn subjects of Great Britain" and irrevocable recognitions of the authority of the assemblies to tax and govern without leave of Parliament. In fact, the charter-rights argument was extremely weak, at least in terms of home rule for all colonies. But so long as it made any sense, the New Englanders, for whom Otis was a typical spokesman, appealed repeatedly to their sacred charters.

It would indeed seem very hard and severe, for those of the colonists, who have charters, with peculiar priviledges, to loose them. They were given to their ancestors, in consideration of their sufferings and merit, in discovering and settling America. Our fore-fathers were soon worn away in the toils of hard labour on their little plantations, and in

war with the Savages. They thought they were earning a
sure inheritance for their posterity. Could they imagine it
would ever be tho't just to deprive them or theirs of their
charter priviledges!

A much broader yet equally conservative footing on
which to stand and resist oppressive acts of Parliament
was the British Constitution and British rights—the
former still that "glorious fabrick," "that noble constitution—the envy and terror of Europe," the latter still "the
invaluable Rights of Englishmen. . . . Rights! which no
Time, no Contract, no Climate can diminish!" Not until
the final resort to arms did Americans waver in their
allegiance to the government and liberties they enjoyed
as "descendants of free-born Britons." Paine's open assault
on "the so much boasted constitution of England" was
perhaps the most radical section in *Common Sense*. Almost all other colonists were proud to live with Rev.
Gad Hitchcock under governments that were "nearly
copies of the happy British original," or of enjoying with
John Adams "the British constitution in greater purity
and perfection than they do in England." Magna Charta,
the Glorious Revolution, and other memorable documents and events in the story of English liberty were
called upon for support. The Bill of Rights, the Habeas
Corpus Act, and the Petition of Right were reprinted
widely for popular edification. Nowhere was the conservative temper of colonial polemics more evident than
in this loyal, desperate veneration of a form of government whose chief distinction was its undoubted antiquity.
Whether conservative or radical, few Americans ever
disagreed with John Witherspoon's judgment:

It is proper to observe, that the British settlements have
been improved in a proportion far beyond the settlements of

other European nations. To what can this be ascribed? Not to the climate, for they are of all climates; not to the people, for they are a mixture of all nations. It must therefore be resolved singly into the degree of British liberty which they brought from home, and which pervaded more or less their several constitutions.

Finally, in their never-ending expression of "the warmest sentiments of affection and duty to his majesty's person and government" and attachment "to the present happy establishment of the protestant succession," the colonists revealed their deep-seated political conservatism. Not until months after the shooting war had begun did they turn away sadly from their conviction that the house of Hanover was "amongst the choicest of God's providential gifts to Great-Britain and the British Colonies." Rarely did a writer so much as hint that the oppressive acts of Parliament or coercions of the ministry could be laid at the King's door. In their anxiety to preserve the blessings of a cherished constitutional monarchy, the colonists ignored almost wilfully the plain fact of the King's eager association in the policy of tighter imperial control. Even after Lexington and Concord the Massachusetts Provincial Congress could declare:

These, brethren, are marks of ministerial vengeance against this colony, for refusing, with her sister colonies, a submission to slavery; but they have not yet detached us from our royal sovereign. We profess to be his loyal and dutiful subjects, and so hardly dealt with as we have been, are still ready, with our lives and fortunes, to defend his person, family, crown and dignity.

Colonial propagandists contributed materially to the show of unanimity on this issue. Yet the propagandists themselves would have been the first to admit that the depth of American feeling for the monarchy and its incumbent made possible their fabrication of "the very model of a patriot king." Simple folk and propagandists alike were careful to maintain the crucial distinction between King and ministry well stated by Rev. Jacob Duché:

Have we not repeatedly and solemnly professed an inviolable loyalty to the person, power, and dignity of our sovereign, and unanimously declared, that it is not with him we contend, but with an envious cloud of false witnesses, that surround his throne, and intercept the sunshine of his favor from our oppressed land?

English Whigs were taken somewhat aback by the warmth of colonial fealty, especially when Hamilton, Wilson, and others seemed ready to grant the King wide powers of government. But Americans were Whigs, not Tories. They had no intention of blowing up the royal prerogative into a potential tyranny. The King so loved and exalted was a constitutional monarch. His chief business was to protect the Americans from parliamentary or ministerial oppression. His prerogative was a check on power rather than power itself. And if ever he should step out of his constitutional role, the remedy, according to a writer in the *Virginia Gazette* in 1773, was that reserved for all tyrant kings:

Virginians, you have nothing to fear, for Centuries to come, while you continue under the Protection of the Crown. You are defended against its Encroachments by the Power you have derived from the People. Should the King of Britain ever invade your Rights, he ceases, according to the British Constitution, to be King of the Dominion of Virginia.

Not until 1776 and *Common Sense* did Americans wake from their dream of a patriot king.

It need only be added in passing—for we shall return to this point in a few pages—that a conservatism in political speculation matched this conservatism in political debate. However radical Revolutionary principles may have seemed to the rest of the world, in the minds of the colonists they were thoroughly preservative and respectful of the past. The explanation is, of course, that the American past—at least as Americans liked to read it—displayed a condition of human liberty and constitutional government that the rest of the world could only long for or detest. The political thought of this revolution was designed to preserve a world that had already been made over to the satisfaction of all reasonable men.

Sense of Destiny. Pamphleteers and orators had their eyes on the future as well as the past. Having called upon his listeners to "look back to the times of ancient virtue and renown," Provost Smith reminded them that they were ancestors as well as descendants. It was entirely up to them whether they should be venerated, despised, or forgotten:

Look forward also to distant posterity. Figure to yourselves millions and millions to spring from your loins, who may be born *freemen* or *slaves,* as Heaven shall now approve or reject your councils. Think, that on you it may depend, whether this great country, in ages hence, shall be filled and adorned with a virtuous and inlightened people; enjoying *Liberty* and all its concomitant blessings . . . or covered with a race of men more contemptible than the savages that roam the wilderness.

All American writers sounded the note of destiny, reminding fellow countrymen that their deeds would determine the fate and their words inspire the hearts of generations of free men yet unborn. It was the sort of exhortation in which Tom Paine excelled—repeated by his less eloquent but no less convinced colleagues in thousands of sermons and letters—that raised a peevish quarrel over unpopular taxes to an epic struggle over the future of a continent:

The Sun never shined on a cause of greater worth. 'Tis not the affair of a City, a County, a Province, or a Kingdom; but of a Continent—of at least one eighth part of the habitable Globe. 'Tis not the concern of a day, a year, or an age; posterity are virtually involved in the contest, and will be more or less affected even to the end of time, by the proceedings now. Now is the seed-time of Continental union, faith and honour.

Faith in the transcendent importance of the American cause reached its peak of conviction in the concept of the American Mission. The leaders of the Revolution, like the prophets of ancient Israel, were convinced that God had singled out their nation for a destiny far higher than their own prosperity and greatness. "The Revolution," wrote John Witherspoon, was "an important aera in the history of mankind," for it was now to be determined—in the best possible laboratory and with the best possible materials—whether free government could be made reality or must remain a cruel will-o'-the-wisp. America would have other missions: For one thing, it was "a country marked out by the great *God* of nature as a receptacle for distress." But its central mission was to be the testing-ground of freedom. Washington caught the solemnity of this truth in his first inaugural address:

The preservation of the sacred fire of liberty and the destiny of the republican model of government are justly considered, perhaps, as *deeply*, as *finally*, staked on the experiment intrusted to the hands of the American people.

The American Mission was plainly a decisive factor in the shaping of Revolutionary political thought, for it drove the colonists beyond charter and Constitution to claim sanction for their actions in the great principles of natural justice. The appeal to the universal doctrines of natural law and natural rights came easily to a people who believed words like these, preached in 1778 by Rev. Phillips Payson:

To anticipate the future glory of America from our present hopes and prospects is ravishing and transporting to the mind. In this light we behold our country, beyond the reach of all oppressors, under the great charter of independence, enjoying the purest liberty; beautiful and strong in its union; the envy of tyrants and devils, but the delight of God and all good men; a refuge to the oppressed; the joy of the earth; each state happy in a wise model of government, and abounding with wise men, patriots, and heroes; the strength and abilities of the whole continent, collected in a grave and venerable council, at the head of all, seeking and promoting the good of the present and future generations. Hail, my happy country, saved of the Lord! Happy land, emerged from the deluges of the Old World drowned in luxury and lewd excess! Hail, happy posterity, that shall reap the peaceful fruits of our sufferings, fatigues, and wars!

This conviction of a higher destiny had much to do with the popularity of American political thought among liberty-minded men in England and France. America became an influential center of political speculation in the last three decades of the eighteenth century because American writers, in a burst of happy prophecy, took the grand view of their country's future.

FOUR

The American Consensus

OCCASIONAL, propagandistic, legalistic, factual, conservative, conscious of destiny—these words catch the quality of political argument in the years of the American Revolution. Two final characteristics, perhaps the most significant for our purposes, remain to be noted.

The first was the habit, in which most American writers indulged to excess, of "recurring to first principles," of appealing to basic doctrines of political theory to support legal, factual, and constitutional arguments. Few men were willing to argue about a specific issue—deny the wisdom of the Stamp Act, defend an editor against charges of libel, protest the landing of tea, interpret the Massachusetts Charter, condemn the quartering of troops in New York—without first calling upon rules of justice that were considered to apply to all men everywhere. These rules, of course, were the ancient body of political assumptions known as natural law and natural rights. The great political philosophy of the Western world enjoyed one of its proudest seasons in this time of resistance and revolution. If the Americans added few novel twists of their own to this philosophy, they gave it a unique vogue among men of all ranks and callings. Few people in history have been so devoted to a "party line" that had no sanction other than its appeal to free minds; few people have made such effective use of the recourse to first principles.

The reasons for the popularity of natural law and natural rights are not difficult to understand. This philosophy gave men of all colonies and national origins a common ground on which to stand and defy ministerial tyranny. It came naturally to colonial advocates who could see that they were getting nowhere with appeals to the charters, English rights, and simple expediency. "It has often mortified me," a gentleman masquerading as Benevolus wrote to the New Jersey Assembly in early 1775,

to hear our warmest advocates for liberty (tho' with the best design) recurring to doubtful constitutions, charters, acts of Parliament, and public faith, as the foundations of our reasonable and rightful claims—These, at best, can be but declaratory of those rights—The true foundation of American liberty, is in human nature.

The universality of natural law gave Americans a strong sense of fellowship with all men struggling to be free, while its antiquity placed them in a great chain of heroes and philosophers stretching back through their own ancestors to the beginnings of Western history. Natural law and rights, John Adams wrote, "are what are called revolution principles."

They are the principles of Aristotle and Plato, of Livy and Cicero, and Sidney, Harrington, and Locke; the principles of nature and eternal reason; the principles on which the whole government over us now stands. It is therefore aston-

ishing, if any thing can be so, that writers, who call themselves friends of government, should in this age and country
be so inconsistent with themselves, so indiscreet, so immodest,
as to insinuate a doubt concerning them.

In point of fact, few "friends of government"—no matter where they stood in the debate over the authority of
Parliament—had any doubt that "first principles" lay at
the foundation of politics, or had any doubt that it was
important to proclaim them loudly and confidently.

The second was the existence of what I have called,
with some trepidation lest the phrase be misunderstood,
the American "party line." What is essential for students
of our intellectual history to remember is that there were
few deviationists from this line, that there was an over-
powering consensus of political principle among the men
of the Revolution. Some spokesmen for the patriot cause
saluted natural law and natural rights only in passing;
others demonstrated that the question was, after all, one
of free choice by expressing irregular opinions of the
nature of man or origin of government. But all American
publicists—whether celebrated or anonymous, sophisticated or untutored, speculative or pedestrian—paid devotion of one sort or another to "revolution principles."
Nowhere in patriot literature is there a single direct sug-
gestion that the essentials of this political theory were
unhistorical, illogical, or unsound. Even the Tories, except for bold spirits like Jonathan Boucher, refrained
from attacking it frontally, and even Boucher, if the
tactical situation demanded such talk, could speak of "consent," "constitutional right," and "the great Hampden."
The warmest sort of enemy approval of the American
consensus was expressed in Gentleman Johnny Bur-
goyne's famous letter to Charles Lee of July, 1775:

I am no stranger to the doctrines of Mr. Locke and other of the best advocates for the rights of mankind, upon the compact always implied between the governing and the governed, and the right of resistance in the latter, when the compact shall be so violated as to leave no other means of redress. I look with reverence, almost amounting to idolatry, upon those immortal whigs who adopted and applied such doctrine during part of the reign of Charles the 1st, and in that of James IId.

In political thought, if not in devotion to the patriot cause, "nine tenths of the people" were, as John Adams remarked, "high whigs." To the political thought of high Whiggery the rest of this book will be wholly devoted. As an introduction to the chapters that follow, let me quote at length from four memorable expressions of the common faith. The first, "The Rights of the Colonists," written by James Otis and Samuel Adams and adopted by the Boston town meeting, November 29, 1772, is a reminder that men in the mass subscribed to the principles of the American consensus:

Among the Natural Rights of the Colonists are these First. a Right to *Life;* Secondly to *Liberty;* thirdly to *Property;* together with the Right to support and defend them in the best manner they can—Those are evident Branches of, rather than deductions from the Duty of Self Preservation, commonly called the first Law of Nature—

All Men have a Right to remain in a State of Nature as long as they please: And in case of intollerable Oppression, Civil or Religious, to leave the Society they belong to, and enter into another.—

When Men enter into Society, it is by voluntary consent; and they have a right to demand and insist upon the performance of such conditions, And previous limitations as form an equitable *original compact.*—

Every natural Right not expressly given up or from the nature of a Social Compact necessarily ceded remains.—

All positive and civil laws, should conform as far as possible, to the Law of natural reason and equity.—

As neither reason requires, nor religeon permits the contrary, every Man living in or out of a state of civil society, has a right peaceably and quietly to worship God according to the dictates of his conscience. . . .

The natural liberty of Men by entring into society is abridg'd or restrained so far only as is necessary for the Great end of Society the best good of the whole—

In the state of nature, every man is under God, Judge and sole Judge, of his own rights and the injuries done him: By entering into society, he agrees to an Arbiter or indifferent Judge between him and his neighbours; but he no more renounces his original right, than by taking a cause out of the ordinary course of law, and leaving the decision to Referees or indifferent Arbitrations. . . .

"The natural liberty of man is to be free from any superior power on earth, and not to be under the will or legislative authority of man; but only to have the law of nature for his rule. . . ."

In short it is the greatest absurdity to suppose it in the power of one or any number of men at the entering into society, to renounce their essential natural rights, or the means of preserving those rights when the great end of civil government from the very nature of its institution is for the support, protection and defence of those very rights: the principal of which as is before observed, are life, liberty and property. If men through fear, fraud or mistake, should *in terms* renounce and give up any essential natural right, the eternal law of reason and the great end of society, would absolutely vacate such renunciation; the right to freedom being *the gift* of God Almighty, it is not in the power of Man to alienate this gift, and voluntarily become a slave. . . .

A Common Wealth or state is a body politick or civil society of men, united together to promote their mutual safety and prosperity, by means of their union.

The *absolute Rights* of Englishmen, and all freemen in or out of Civil society, are principally, *personal security personal liberty* and *private property.*

All Persons born in the British American Colonies are by the laws of God and nature, and by the Common law of England, *exclusive of all charters from the Crown,* well Entitled, and by the Acts of the British Parliament are declared to be entitled to all the natural essential, inherent & inseperable Rights Liberties and Privileges of Subjects born in Great Britain, or within the Realm. Among those Rights are the following; which no men or body of men, consistently with their own rights as men and citizens or members of society, can for themselves give up, or take away from others.

First, "The first fundamental positive law of all Commonwealths or States, is the establishing the legislative power; as the first fundamental *natural* law also, which is to govern even the legislative power itself, is the preservation of the Society."

Secondly, The Legislative has no right to absolute arbitrary power over the lives and fortunes of the people. . . .

Thirdly, The supreme power cannot Justly take from any man, any part of his property without his consent, in person or by his Representative.—

These are some of the first principles of natural law & Justice, and the great Barriers of all free states, and of the British Constitution in particular. It is utterly irreconcileable to these principles, and to many other fundamental maxims of the common law, common sense and reason, that a British house of commons, should have a right, at pleasure, to give and grant the property of the Colonists.

The second expression, which is a reminder that the men at the top subscribed to the consensus with the same fervor, is an extract from the famous "Letter to the Inhabitants of the Province of Quebec," drafted by John Dickinson and adopted by Congress October 26, 1774:

The first grand right, is that of the people having a share in their own government by their representatives chosen by themselves, and, in consequence, of being ruled by *laws,* which they themselves approve, not by *edicts of men* over whom they have no controul. This is a bulwark surrounding and defending their property, which by their honest cares and labours they have acquired, so that no portions of it can legally be taken from them, but with their own full and free consent. . . .

The next great right is that of trial by jury. This provides, that neither life, liberty nor property, can be taken from the possessor, until twelve of his unexceptionable countrymen and peers of his vicinage, who from that neighbourhood may reasonably be supposed to be acquainted with his character, and the characters of the witnesses, upon a fair trial, and full enquiry, face to face, in open Court, before as many of the people as chuse to attend, shall pass their sentence upon oath against him. . . .

Another right relates merely to the liberty of the person. If a subject is seized and imprisoned, tho' by order of Government, he may, by virtue of this right, immediately obtain a writ, termed a Habeas Corpus, from a Judge, whose sworn duty it is to grant it, and thereupon procure any illegal restraint to be quickly enquired into and redressed.

A fourth right, is that of holding lands by the tenure of easy rents, and not by rigorous and oppressive services, frequently forcing the possessors from their families and their business, to perform what ought to be done, in all well regulated states, by men hired for the purpose.

The last right we shall mention, regards the freedom of the press. The importance of this consists, besides the advancement of truth, science, morality, and arts in general, in its diffusion of liberal sentiments on the administration of Government, its ready communication of thoughts between subjects, and its consequential promotion of union among them, whereby oppressive officers are shamed or intimidated, into more honourable and just modes of conducting affairs.

These are the invaluable rights, that form a considerable part of our mild system of government; that, sending its equitable energy through all ranks and classes of men, defends the poor from the rich, the weak from the powerful, the industrious from the rapacious, the peaceable from the violent, the tenants from the lords, and all from their superiors.

These are the rights, without which a people cannot be free and happy.

The third, the Virginia Declaration of Rights of June 12, 1776, which was written by George Mason, is an especially important document, for it is unquestionably the most eloquent, celebrated, and influential of all the bills of rights put forth by many of the new states in the first years of self-government:

A Declaration of Rights, made by the Representatives of the good People of Virginia, assembled in full and free Convention, which rights do pertain to them and their posterity as the basis and foundation of government.

I. That all men are by nature equally free and independent, and have certain inherent rights, of which, when they enter into a state of society, they cannot by any compact deprive or divest their posterity; namely, the enjoyment of life and liberty, with the means of acquiring and possessing property, and pursuing and obtaining happiness and safety.

II. That all power is vested in, and consequently derived from, the people; that magistrates are their trustees and servants, and at all times amenable to them.

III. That government is, or ought to be, instituted for the common benefit, protection, and security of the people, nation or community; of all the various modes and forms of government, that is best which is capable of producing the greatest degree of happiness and safety, and is most effectually secured against the danger of maladministration; and that, when a government shall be found inadequate or contrary to these purposes, a majority of the community hath an indubitable, unalienable, and indefeasible right to reform, alter or abolish it, in such manner as shall be judged most conducive to the public weal.

IV. That no man, or set of men, are entitled to exclusive or separate emoluments or privileges from the community but in consideration of public services, which not being descendible, neither ought the offices of magistrate, legislator or judge to be hereditary.

V. That the legislative, executive and judicial powers should be separate and distinct; and that the members thereof may be restrained from oppression, by feeling and participating the burthens of the people, they should, at fixed periods, be reduced to a private station, return into that body from which they were originally taken, and the vacancies be supplied by frequent, certain and regular elections, in which all, or any part or the former members to be again eligible or ineligible, as the laws shall direct.

VI. That all elections ought to be free, and that all men having sufficient evidence of permanent common interest with, and attachment to the community, have the right of suffrage, and cannot be taxed, or deprived of their property for public uses, without their own consent, or that of their representatives so elected, nor bound by any law to which they have not in like manner assented, for the public good.

VII. That all power of suspending laws, or the execution of laws, by any authority, without consent of the representatives of the people, is injurious to their rights, and ought not to be exercised.

VIII. That in all capital or criminal prosecutions a man hath a right to demand the cause and nature of his accusation, to be confronted with the accusers and witnesses, to call for evidence in his favour, and to a speedy trial by an impartial jury of twelve men of his vicinage, without whose unanimous consent he cannot be found guilty; nor can he be compelled to give evidence against himself; that no man be deprived of his liberty, except by the law of the land or the judgment of his peers.

IX. That excessive bail ought not to be required, nor. excessive fines imposed, nor cruel and unusual punishments inflicted.

X. That general warrants, whereby an officer or messenger may be commanded to search suspected places without evidence of a fact committed, or to seize any person or persons not named, or whose offence is not particularly described and supported by evidence, are grievous and oppressive, and ought not to be granted.

XI. That in controversies respecting property, and in suits between man and man, the ancient trial by jury of twelve men is preferable to any other, and ought to be held sacred.

XII. That the freedom of the press is one of the great bulwarks of liberty, and can never be restrained but by despotic governments.

XIII. That a well-regulated militia, composed of the body of the people, trained to arms, is the proper, natural and safe defence of a free State; that standing armies in time of peace should be avoided as dangerous to liberty; and that in all cases the military should be under strict subordination to, and governed by, the civil power.

XIV. That the people have a right to uniform government; and therefore that no government separate from or independent of the government of Virginia ought to be erected or established within the limits thereof.

XV. That no free government, or the blessing of liberty, can be preserved to any people, but by a firm adherence to justice, moderation, temperance, frugality and virtue, and by a frequent recurrence to fundamental principles.

XVI. That religion, or the duty which we owe to our

Creator, and the manner of discharging it, can be directed only by reason and conviction, not by force or violence; and therefore all men are equally entitled to the free exercise of religion, according to the dictates of conscience; and that it is the duty of all to practice Christian forbearance, love and charity towards each other.

The declarations of rights of 1776 remain America's most notable contribution to universal political thought. Through these eloquent statements of the rights of man political theory became political reality. Yet they, as we know, do not stand alone, for they are best understood as reflections of what is still rightly considered the historic statement of the political thought of the American Revolution, a document which, I trust, needs no identification:

We hold these truths to be self-evident, that all men are created equal, that they are endowed by their Creator with certain unalienable Rights, that among these are Life, Liberty, and the pursuit of Happiness. That, to secure these rights, Governments are instituted among Men, deriving their just Powers from the consent of the governed. That, whenever any form of Government becomes destructive of these ends, it is the Right of the People to alter or to abolish it, and to institute new Government, laying its foundation on such Principles, and organizing its Powers in such form, as to them shall seem most likely to effect their Safety and Happiness. Prudence, indeed, will dictate that Governments long established should not be changed for light and transient causes; and, accordingly, all experience hath shewn, that mankind are more disposed to suffer, while evils are sufferable, than to right themselves by abolishing the forms to which they are accustomed. But, when a long train of abuses and usurpations, pursuing invariably the same Object, evinces a design to reduce them under absolute Despotism, it is their right, it is their duty, to throw off such Government, and to provide new Guards for their future Security.

Here, in a few felicitous and frugal words that thunder more loudly with each passing generation, is the American consensus of 1776.

FIVE

*The Sources
of Political Thought*

ALMOST FIFTY YEARS after the event, the author of the Declaration of Independence had this to say in reply to a soft indictment of his performance as one quite lacking in originality:

With respect to our rights, and the acts of the British government contravening those rights, there was but one opinion on this side of the water. All American whigs thought alike on these subjects. When forced, therefore, to resort to arms for redress, an appeal to the tribunal of the world was deemed proper for our justification. This was the object of the Declaration of Independence. Not to find out new principles, or new arguments, never before thought of, not merely to say things which had never been said before; but to place before mankind the common sense of the subject, in terms so plain and firm as to command their assent, and to justify ourselves in the independent stand we are compelled to take. Neither aiming at originality of principle or sentiment, nor yet copied from any particular and previous writing, it was intended to be an expression of the American mind, and to give to that expression the proper tone and spirit called for by the occasion. All its authority rests then on the harmonizing sentiments of the day, whether expressed in conversation, in letters, printed essays, or in the elementary books of public right, as Aristotle, Cicero, Locke, Sidney, &c.

This interesting statement is the best of all possible introductions to a chapter on the sources of Revolutionary political thought. The men of the Revolution were consumers rather than producers of ideas, and Jefferson was simply being more honest in his old age than most of his colleagues had been in their days of wrath.

In particular, Americans were conscious heirs of the noble tradition of natural law. Rome, Israel, the church, the continent, and England had all brought forth great men to affirm the reality of moral restraints on political power, and Americans turned eagerly to these prophets of freedom for philosophical support in the struggle against England. The principles of natural law, which were made concrete in the axioms of Whig constitutionalism, were part of almost everyone's intellectual equipment. No one really had to quote chapter and verse for ideas like the contract and the right to property. But the rules of the game, especially as played in England, required political thinkers to cite their authorities, and this the colonists were entirely willing to do. The men of the Revolution were not slaves to the past they adored; they were selective about the men they quoted and about the ideas they took from any particular man. They searched all literature for words of liberty and refused to let a man's reputation repel or dazzle them. Thus they seized upon Blackstone's homage to natural law and ignored Locke's comments on the supremacy of Parliament. We may separate their main sources into four categories.

The Ancients. The Hebraic, Christian, and classical traditions were all very much alive in the colonies. Spokesmen for liberty in each tradition saw heavy duty in the patriot cause. Dissenting ministers, of course, relied happily on the famous men of the Old and New Testaments. Out of the mouths of prophets and apostles they plucked encouraging words about resistance, liberty, equality, public virtue, patriotism, and higher law. John Allen saluted Micah as a "SON OF LIBERTY," and Samuel Cooper traced the compact back to Joshua and his companions. They did not, however, make use of the church fathers, who were too much the property of Catholicism for these self-conscious Protestants to flaunt in debate. St. Thomas Aquinas might just as well never have written his expositions of higher law.

Among the Greeks to whom learned men like Jefferson and John Adams appealed for support were Herodotus, Thucydides, Plutarch, and Polybius. Aristotle enjoyed only a slight vogue, and Plato was virtually ignored. Although Dickinson could quote Sophocles on "the unwritten law divine, immutable, eternal" in a convincing manner, most authors used the ancient Greeks simply for window-dressing. The history of the Greek leagues was more instructive to colonial writers than the arguments of Greek philosophers. The Romans were much more useful to the patriot cause, especially Cicero for his exposition of natural law, Tacitus for his defense of a simple, agrarian society, and the imperial lawyers for their insistence on the existence of a higher law. But they, too, were men who confirmed the colonists in old convictions rather than taught them anything new. Americans would have believed just as vigorously in the beauties of public morality had Cato and the Gracchi never lived.

English Libertarians. In no instance did the resisting colonists prove themselves such faithful children of England as in their sweeping reliance on English political thinkers. Patriot spokesmen dug deep in the libraries of their fathers to find any Englishman who could be quoted in support of the cause. Common-law jurists, liberal ecclesiastics, seventeenth-century republicans, eighteenth-century Whigs, and even learned Tories were called to judgment. The one mildly surprising omission from the catalogue of English authorities was the complete boycott of the Levellers and Diggers of the seventeenth century. Lilburne, Winstanley, Overton, and the rest never appear in the literature of the Revolution. Those colonists who knew their work were probably aware that no purpose would be served by dragging them into the argument. And in any case, the American consensus of political ideas was as far to the right of the Levellers as it was to the left of Jacobite exponents of divine right and passive obedience. Two other English thinkers whom the Americans refused to touch were Hobbes and Filmer. If they appear at all in Revolutionary literature, it is only to serve as straw men for patriots to ridicule and knock down. David Hume, on the other hand, was treated with some respect, especially by young Alexander Hamilton and conservative John Dickinson.

It is not easy to separate the English libertarians into major and minor prophets of the American cause, but several men do stand out as thinkers whom the colonists seem to have read and pondered with special care: John Locke, of whom more in a moment; Algernon Sidney, still the *beau idéal* of the American republicans; Sir Edward Coke, "that great luminary of the law," the human embodiment of common law, Magna Charta, and constitutionalism; Lord Bolingbroke, of whom John Adams observed tartly, "[His] knowledge of the constitution will not be disputed, whatever may be justly said of his religion and his morals"; and Thomas Gordon and John Trenchard, whose *Cato's Letters* retained the wide audience in this nation of Whigs that they had built up in the colonial period.

In the second rank, according to actual use of their words and ideas, were such diverse British thinkers as Joseph Addison, the Marquis of Halifax, Lord John Somers, Henry Care, Richard Hooker, John Milton, Francis Hutcheson, Benjamin Hoadly, Marchamont Nedham, Henry Neville, Christopher St. Germain, George Buchanan, Thomas Bradbury, Robert Dodsley, John Knox, Sir John Hawles, Bishop Burnet, William Molineux, William Wollaston, and James Harrington. Works of Somers, Care, Buchanan, Bradbury, Dodsley, Knox, and Hawles were reprinted in the colonies in the decade before independence. St. Germain's sixteenth-century legal treatise *Doctor and Student* was a favorite of Jefferson's, and Harrington's *Oceana* helped shape the mettlesome mind of John Adams. Milton is worth mentioning only because of the rarity with which he was quoted; it would almost seem that a conspiracy had been raised against him. Jurists other than Coke who were used with regularity were Bracton, Fortescue, Hale, Holt, Kames, and Bacon.

The influence of John Locke's second treatise *Of Civil Government* must be more carefully weighed. Locke has always been considered the supreme if not indeed exclusive source of Revolutionary ideas. Other men's works may have been cited, we are told, but Locke's were studied: He was the one genuine philosophical ancestor of the Adamses, Jefferson, and the political preachers, the man acclaimed and echoed by all America, according to a writer in the *Pennsylvania Gazette*, as "the finest reasoner, and best writer on government, that this or any other age has produced." Locke was hardly less the theoretical father of the American Revolution than Marx of the Russian. But is this true?

It is difficult to estimate the debt owed to Locke by patriot thinkers, yet the unmistakable impression one gets from roaming through the entire range of Revolutionary literature is that he was definitely not so important a figure as we have hitherto assumed. There is no evidence that his treatise (first printed in America in 1773) sold any better than a half-dozen other books that said pretty much the same thing, and until 1774 his name was mentioned only rarely in the columns of even the most radical newspapers. In hundreds of Whiggish pamphlets and letters he is not quoted at all; in other hundreds he appears as one of four or five English and Continental sources. Perhaps ninety per cent of the quotations from *Civil Government* are limited to a few overworked passages about property and legislation, and his famous discussion of "the dissolution of government" is hardly used at all. Many thoughtful colonists turned away from his confusions and omissions to summon other thinkers to testify about the origin of government and substance of natural law.

This must not be taken to mean that Locke lacked stature with the learned or popularity with the public. He had a very special place in American affections. He was, in the admiring view of William Livingston,

Sagacious *Locke,* by providence design'd
T'exalt, instruct, and rectify the mind.

Nathaniel Ames spoke the minds of a great many people in 1775, when he wrote in his almanac: "As it is unpardonable for a Navigator to be without his charts, so it is for a *Senator* to be without HIS, which is Lock's 'Essay on Government.'" A great many others, however, seemed to prefer the writings of Burlamaqui or Vattel or even Blackstone as master charts of the rights of man. The natural-law philosophy had long held sway in the Western world, and a colonist in search of first principles could have turned to any one of a score of political theorists and have been completely satisfied. John Wise, the most vocal and explicit of all natural-law thinkers in the colonial period, read his lessons with Pufendorf and never even mentioned Locke. If Locke looms above the other great men of this ancient school, if he is the one author whom Tories delighted to throw back at patriot publicists, it is probably because of one very practical rather than philosophical reason: He was a famous, almost unassailable English philosopher who had glorified a rebellion of Englishmen against an English king. Despite his inconsistencies and omissions, despite his failure to give the ancient line any really new twist, he was therefore the most popular source of Revolutionary ideas. As such he was *primus inter pares,* not the lonely oracle of the American cause.

Continental Libertarians. Although many references in Revolutionary literature to European authors were window-dressing of the most obvious sort, at least four Continental philosophers were studied with care and quoted with confidence: Emmerich de Vattel, a name to be flung about as confidently as that of Locke or Sidney; Baron Pufendorf, whose name turns up repeatedly in the most improbable places; Jean Jacques Burlamaqui, a particular favorite of James Wilson and John Dickinson; and the Baron de Montesquieu, whom every literate colonist could quote to advantage, and whose exposition of the separation of powers was already making perfect sense to American minds. It would be hard to fix the precise responsibility of any one of these men for any one leading principle of colonial thought, except in the case of Montesquieu's doctrine of the separation of powers and Burlamaqui's emphasis on happiness as a right of man and an object of government. They all had the same message for the men of the Revolution: that government could be limited, that men could be free, that a king could be unseated for playing the tyrant. Other Continentals who appear occasionally, but only occasionally, in Revolutionary tracts are Grotius, Jean Domat, Barbeyrac, Voltaire, and Beccaria. John Adams was one of the few colonists who dared or cared to use Machiavelli. Rousseau, far from being an important source of the Declaration of Independence, was a minor figure of whom precious few traces can be found. Indeed, Rousseau's whole approach to man, society, and government ran counter to the basic principles of American Revolutionary thought. The men of 1776 went to the Continent to seek help for the English Whigs, not to learn any new and unsettling ideas.

Contemporary Englishmen. Revolutionary pamphleteers and orators drew heavy intellectual support from two classes of contemporary Englishmen: a small band of Whig statesmen who spoke up manfully for American

rights, and an even smaller band of radicals who clung
to the doctrine of natural rights in the face of a nation
grown weary of Locke and Sidney. The most widely
quoted in the first group were Edmund Burke, Colonel
Barré, Lord Camden, Bishop Shipley, General Conway,
Charles James Fox, Governor Johnstone, and above all
the elder Pitt. Men like Pitt and Barré looked upon the
colonists' cause as their cause, and their speeches in the
Whig tradition were reprinted, studied, and quoted
wherever men debated their liberties in the years after
the Stamp Act. Pitt, "glorious and immortal," the "guard-
ian of America," was the idol of the colonies. His eloquent arguments against taxation without representation
were repaid in full measure by a grateful people. Ships,
towns, and babies bore the proud name of Pitt; preachers,
orators, and poets celebrated his Roman virtues. In the
words of a correspondent in the *Portsmouth Mercury*
in 1766:

> I thank thee, Pitt, for all thy glorious Strife
> Against the Foes of LIBERTY and Life.

In the same year a Son of Liberty in Bristol County,
Massachusetts, paid him the ultimate tribute of identification with English liberty:

> Our Toast in general is,—*Magna Charta*,—the *British
> Constitution*,—PITT and Liberty forever!

The most prominent members of the second category
were Richard Price, James Burgh, Joseph Priestley,
Granville Sharp, Catherine Macauley, John Cartwright,
David Hartley the younger, and the unknown authors
of the *Letters of Junius* and *The Crisis*. Reprints of
their works appeared everywhere in the colonies. Price's

Observations on the Nature of Civil Liberty and *The Crisis* were especially popular with colonial debaters, the former for bringing Locke up to date, the latter for its savage attacks on King and Parliament and its justification of the right of resistance. John Wilkes and the Irish patriot Dr. Charles Lucas were other radicals whose words appeared repeatedly in colonial pamphlets and letters. Few American leaders knew just what to make of Wilkes as a man, but many made a great deal of his arguments for parliamentary privilege and the liberty of the subject. It should nevertheless be plain that one friendly observation of Pitt or Burke was worth more to American pamphleteers than a hundred pages of Price or the entire works of Wilkes. Not until the argument shifted substantially away from English rights and over to natural justice did Price and Priestley influence American minds.

One other contemporary Englishman, a man who defies easy classification, remains to be mentioned: Sir William Blackstone, the great Tory jurist. The publication of his *Commentaries* in Philadelphia in 1771 was a major event in American intellectual history. Blackstone's huge influence on American law is, of course, well known; what is not so well known was his high standing as political thinker with men like Wilson, Hamilton, Dickinson, and Otis. Blackstone was almost as popular among politicians as among lawyers, probably because the one group included so many of the other—and, vice versa. The Americans read the eclectic *Commentaries* in a shrewdly selective manner, citing this oracle repeatedly and effectively in support of all manner of Whiggish doctrines. Two of the most popular borrowings from English political literature were Black-

stone's memorable salutes to natural law and natural
liberty. The *Commentaries* were also an important secondary outlet for the teachings of Locke and Burlamaqui.

The American spokesmen went everywhere, even to
the Koran, for refinements of political theory and par-
ticulars of public dispute that would aid them in their
struggle against parliamentary power—everywhere, that
is to say, but to their own colonial ancestors. One may
search almost in vain through the literature of the Revolution for a single significant quotation from such major
luminaries of colonial political thought as Thomas
Hooker, of Hartford, Roger Williams, of Providence,
and John Wise, of Ipswich, or from such minor luminaries as the long line of preachers—men like Jared Eliot,
John Barnard, Abraham Williams, Elisha Williams, Ebenezer Pemberton, Noah Hobart, and John Woodward
—who had advertised the beauties of natural liberty and
constitutional government in the annual election sermons in Connecticut and Massachusetts. A few scraps
from Hooker's desolate farewell sermon to England in
1633 appeared in the *New-Hampshire Gazette,* June 15,
1776, a few offhand references to Williams in Stephen
Hopkins's account of the first settlers in Rhode Island,
which was printed in the *Providence Gazette* in early
1765. Wise's two most celebrated tracts—*The Churches'
Quarrel Espoused* (1710) and *A Vindication of the Government of New-England Churches* (1717)—were reprinted in 1772, and were then ignored completely by
Revolutionary pamphleteers. Increase Mather's *Narrative of the Miseries . . . in the Tyrannic Reign of Sir
Edmond Andros,* Cotton Mather's *The Good Old Ways,*
John Peter Zenger's *Brief Narrative* of his trial for libel

(which carried Andrew Hamilton's famous speech), and Jeremiah Dummer's *Defence of the New-England Charters* were all reprinted for special audiences and obvious reasons, but no colonial writer was ever called to bear witness—as so many Americans had borne witness almost from the time of the first settlements—to the sanctity of the social contract or the perseverance of the right of resistance. Thanks especially to the politicians and preachers of the first half of the eighteenth century, the colonies in 1765 were the world's most fertile ground of the liberating ideas of Locke, Sidney, Pufendorf, and Grotius, as well as of Aristotle and Cicero. Since there was not, however, much point in throwing the words of Noah Hobart into the great debate with the British ministry when one had the words of John Locke right at hand, the whole body of early American thought went almost completely unused.

Yet if men argued for religious liberty without summoning the shade of Roger Williams, if they described the contract without rehearsing the powerful thoughts of John Wise, if they proclaimed the right to depose a tyrant king without quoting Jonathan Mayhew's factitious *Discourse Concerning Unlimited Submission* of 1750, this did not mean that these early American thinkers and their lesser colleagues had written and preached in vain. Quite the contrary, Wise and his fellows had helped create a nation of Whigs for whom the appeal to Locke and Burlamaqui was a completely natural performance. Thanks to the colonial political thinkers, the men of the Revolution were devoted heart and mind to the great traditions of Whiggery and natural justice.

Two

THE RIGHTS OF MAN

*N*ever was there a People," a colonist wrote in 1768, "whom it more immediately concerned to search into the Nature and Extent of their Rights and Privileges than it does the people of America at this Day." Never was there a people for whom advice of this kind was less necessary. Americans searched eagerly into the nature and extent of their rights and privileges; they searched, too, for basic principles that would justify these rights and give them substance.

The principles in which they placed their special trust were, as we have learned, those of the oldest of libertarian philosophies, the school of natural law. The practical purpose of the colonists was to limit the power of Parliament, and like all men with the slightest feeling for abstract justice, they sought limits more universal than those staked out in laws, charters, and constitutions. The great philosophy that preached the reality of moral restraints on power had always been a part of their Anglo-Christian heritage. Now, in their time of trial, the colonists summoned it to their defense. The eloquence of the patriot leaders changed this philosophy, in the words of Lord Bryce, from "a commonplace of morality" to "a mass of dynamite," and with this dynamite they proceeded to blow up an empire.

As we turn to survey the political thought of the Revolution, we must keep one fact clearly in mind: The progression of ideas through the chapters that follow is the result of a modern attempt to bring order out of the writings of men who had neither time nor predilection for ordered exposition. No Revolutionary thinker presented his views in this particular form. Indeed, no one man even touched upon all the ideas that we are to discuss in these pages. The political faith that sustained the Revolution was the work of many men, and only through an intensely ordered rendering of a protean literature can one hope to make clear the principles upon which a majority agreed. The organization of Parts II and III follows the lead of Revolutionary authors in presenting these principles in the two familiar contexts of man and government. The state of nature, the law of nature, and the nature and rights of man are the subjects of inquiry in Part II. The origin, purpose, nature, structure, and moral basis of government are the concern of Part III. The many ideas that appear in both parts are evidence of the Revolutionary assumption that man without government was almost impossible to imagine.

SIX

The State of Nature
and the Law of Nature

THE STATE OF NATURE—described by Locke as the state of "men living together according to reason without a common superior on earth, with authority to judge between them"—was the point of reference around which Revolutionary thinkers grouped the principles of their political thought. The state of nature was, of course, an old concept, and men raised in the tradition of natural law could accept and use it without feeling any urge to subject it to critical analysis. Most American thinkers were content to mention the state of nature in a sentence or two, then move on briskly to consider those rights which men could be said to enjoy because they had once lived in it. An author writing under the pseudonym Spartanus in the *New-Hampshire Gazette*, June 15, 1776, made one of the few attempts to describe this state:

In the days of Adam and Noah, every man had an equal right to the unoccupied earth, which God said he had given

to the children of men. The whole world was before them,
there was much more land than they could occupy or enjoy.
—Each man had a right to occupy new land where he
pleased, and to take wild beasts by hunting. This was what
civilians call a state of nature. In this state every man had a
right to enjoy himself, a right to his enclosure, to what he
took in hunting, and to feed his flocks where he pleased, so
that in any of these, he did not interfere with any pre-oc-
cupant. In such a state every man had a right to defend himself and repel injuries, as he thought best. . . . Every man
had an equal right to judge between himself & his neighbour,
and to do that which was right in his own eyes.

Samuel Cooke, in his election sermon of 1770, was
another who elaborated upon the state of nature. Indeed,
it would seem that he had two such states in mind:

In a pure state of nature, government is in a great measure unnecessary. Private property in that state is inconsider-
able. Men need no arbiter to determine their rights; they
covet only a bare support; their stock is but the subsistence
of a day; the uncultivated deserts are their habitations, and
they carry their all with them in their frequent removes.
They are each one a law to himself, which in general, is of
force sufficient for their security in that course of life.
It is far otherwise when mankind are formed into collective bodies, or a social state of life. Here, their frequent
mutual intercourse, in a degree, necessarily leads them to
different apprehensions respecting their several rights, even
where their intentions are upright. Temptations to injustice
and violence increase, and the occasions of them multiply in
proportion to the increase and opulence of the society. The
laws of nature, though enforced by divine revelation, which
bind the conscience of the upright, prove insufficient to
restrain the sons of violence, who have not the fear of God
before their eyes.

The true state of nature, that is to say, was simply the condition of no positive law and no formal government that preceded the organization of the political community. A few writers followed Hobbes in describing this state—among them Rev. John Hurt in 1777:

The miseries of the state of nature are so evident, that there is no occasion to display them; every man is sensible that violence, rapine, and slaughter must be continually practised where no restraints are provided to curb the inordinancy of self-affection.

Most, however, agreed with Locke that it was "a state of peace, good-will, mutual assistance, and preservation." All were willing to go one step further with Locke and assert that, although most men in the state of nature were inclined to respect the persons and properties of other men, the want of a superior power to adjust honest differences of opinion and "restrain the sons of violence" rendered it a very precarious existence. The state of nature, like natural man, had much in it that was good, much that was bad. However pleasing the prospect, few men would refuse to abandon it, even fewer seek to return to it. It was a state, Theophilus Parsons insisted, perhaps "more excellent than that, in which men are meanly submissive to the haughty will of an imperious tyrant," but men would go back to it only to clear the ground for a new government.

It is impossible to say just how seriously the colonists believed in the state of nature as a fact of history. Certainly Americans had more right than most people to talk of the state of nature as if it had been or could be a real situation. The spokesman of the Revolution used this phrase to describe these situations of historical fact: the condition of no government in prehistoric or Biblical times; the situation facing the Pilgrim fathers in Provincetown harbor in 1620 and other unorganized or unauthorized settlements throughout the colonial period; the state of the colonies in 1775, especially after the King had dissolved the compact by sending troops against them; and, following Locke, the relations to one another of "governments all through the world." This was, after all, long before the days of cultural anthropology and social history, and a belief in the state of nature as a fact in the past was perfectly consistent with learning or intelligence, especially since all but a tiny fraction of American thinkers seemed to consider this state a pre-political rather than pre-social phenomenon. For men as different in approach as James Otis and Rev. Samuel Cooke society without government—rather than men without society —was the real state of nature.

Most American thinkers were more interested in the state of nature as logical hypothesis than as chronological fact. It was far more convenient for them to assume its existence than to describe its outlines, and certainly such an assumption called for no explanation from men raised in the Anglo-Christian tradition. The state of nature served as a logical antecedent to at least five major principles of Revolutionary thought, since it permitted the colonists to:

proclaim the prior existence and therefore prior validity of the law of nature, the system of natural justice that commands men to love, assist, and respect one another;

describe man's basic nature, by calling attention to

those qualities of character he possesses before and despite government or society;

describe man's basic rights, which are therefore considered the gifts of God or nature and not of the community;

In a state of nature, no man had any *moral* power to deprive another of his life, limbs, property, or liberty; nor the least authority to command or exact obedience from him (Alexander Hamilton).

In a state of nature, every man had the sovereign controul over his own person. He might also have, in that state, a qualified property. . . . Over this qualified property every man in a state of nature had also a sovereign control (Theophilus Parsons).

No man in the State of Nature can justly take Anothers Property without his Consent (Samuel Adams).

Man, in a state of nature, has undoubtedly a right to speak and act without controul (A Freeborn American, *Boston Gazette*, 1767).

demonstrate the clear necessity of government based on principles of freedom;

As in a state of nature much happiness cannot be enjoyed by individuals, so it has been conformable to the inclinations of almost all men, to enter into a political society so constituted, as to remove the inconveniences they were obliged to submit to in their former state, and, at the same time, to retain all those natural rights, the enjoyment of which would be consistent with the nature of a free government, and the necessary subordination to the supreme power of the state (Theophilus Parsons).

and finally, give a mechanistic explanation of the origin of government, in order to free men from the past and let them build new political institutions to suit themselves. "We often read," Thomas Dawes, Jr., declaimed,

of the original contract, and of mankind, in the early ages, passing from a state of nature to immediate civilization. But *what eye* could penetrate through gothic night and barbarous fable to that remote period. Such an eye, perhaps, was present, when the Deity conceived the universe and fixed his compass upon the great deep.

And yet the people of Massachusetts have reduced to practice the wonderful theory. A numerous people have convened in a state of nature, and, like *our ideas* of the patriarchs, have deputed a few fathers of the land to draw up for them a glorious covenant. It has been drawn. The people have signed it with rapture, and have, thereby, bartered, among themselves, an easy degree of obedience for the highest possible civil happiness.

For men anxious to recur to first principles of natural justice the state of nature was a prime philosophical assumption. The dictates of a theory concerned with limits on political power in behalf of individual liberty demanded that men and their rights be declared logically and chronologically anterior to the organized community. Whatever else it was, the pre-political state of nature was an extremely handy point of reference.

The Stamp Act was resisted, the Declaration of Independence written, the Constitution adopted, and the Republic launched in an age when most men in the West, whether subtle or simple, believed unequivocally in higher law, generally called "the law of nature." If a few men like Jeremy Bentham doubted or denied, most political thinkers—in America, all political thinkers—assumed the existence and applicability of "the Laws of Nature and of Nature's God." The colonists realized that they were the latest heirs of a political tradition unrivaled in age and universality. By the time the law of nature had come into their hands, it had assumed many different shapes in the service of many different peoples and purposes. Greek philosophers, Roman jurists, Church fathers, medieval scholastics, Protestant reformers, Continental and English liberals—all these and many others had made rich contributions to the doctrine of natural law. And all had agreed, no matter what their special interpretation of its content and dictates, that it placed some sort of moral restriction on political power, indeed on all human activity. To understand the place of natural law in Revolutionary thought we must seek brief answers to these questions: What did the colonists consider to be its source? How did they define it? What did it actually mean in terms of their system of political thought?

Colonial opinion of the ultimate source of higher law divided into three fairly distinct categories. One group of men held it be of immediately divine origin. For them the higher law was, as Rev. Eliphalet Williams of Hartford told the Connecticut legislature in 1769, "the law of God, eternal and immutable." New England preachers, at least the more conservative of them, were the leading members of this group, but it was by no means confined to clerical thinkers. James Otis, for example, considered the law of nature to be "the *unchangeable will of God,* the author of nature, whose laws never vary." For most of these thinkers, if not necessarily for Otis, the commands of higher law were to be found primarily in Scripture. Since the great men of Israel had commanded a variety of things, Eliphalet Williams's law of God was just about as flexible as Samuel Adams's law of nature.

A second group sought, in the tradition of Cicero and Grotius, to secularize higher law. Although they could not quite eliminate the touch of divinity, they were able to thrust God well into the background. Such rationalists in religion as John Adams and Jefferson were willing to concede that God—not necessarily the Christian God —had set the grand machine of nature in motion, but they added quickly that the laws governing this machine had by now become "natural" in the strictest sense: They were at once cause, effect, and expression of nature, an order of things that functioned without divine intervention. Even if God had decreed this order in His original omnipotence, He could no longer tamper with it. Indeed He, too, was bound to respect and follow its laws. The laws of nature that controlled the actions of men were as certain and imperative as those which controlled the movement of the spheres. They were part of the pattern of nature itself, to be discovered by men, whether Christians or pagans, through the use of right reason. Many thinkers, of course, appealed to both "God and nature," a sort of holy duality, but these must be classed finally as believers in natural as contrasted with purely divine law. Reason rather than revelation was their means of discovering the dictates of higher law.

Cornelia Le Boutillier has argued with some persuasiveness that a few key political thinkers adopted a utilitarian rather than metaphysical approach to higher law. When men like James Wilson spoke of the law of nature, we are told, they "appear . . . to have meant, not a transcendental essence, but a practical plan . . . to make possible individual, free, righteous development within a happy and prosperous commonwealth." History, not God or nature, was the source of higher law; experience, not revelation or reason, taught men its commands and penalties. Whether Wilson or any other like-minded colonist was this much of a utilitarian is debatable, but it can be argued that one strong group of American thinkers looked upon the history of liberty and tyranny as the true source of those rules of natural justice which Parliament seemed bent on violating. The higher law that limited political power was simply an experience-proved boundary "built up in the minds of freedom-loving men—not always the same, perhaps, but always on the alert—beyond which it is not safe for governments to go." *Weltgeschichte ist Weltgericht:* History has a way of punishing those men who disregard its lessons in political freedom.

The colonists revealed the derivative quality of their political thought by quoting English and Continental definitions of the law of nature rather than seeking to define it for themselves. While Locke, Pufendorf, Vattel, and Burlamaqui were all called into service for this purpose, Sir William Blackstone's definition was probably the best known and most widely cited. No young man after 1771 could become a lawyer without reading these words:

Man, considered as a creature, must necessarily be subject to the laws of his creator, for he is entirely a dependent being. . . . And consequently, as man depends absolutely upon his maker for every thing, it is necessary that he should in all points conform to his maker's will.

This will of his maker is called the law of nature. For as

God, when he created matter, and endued it with a principle of mobility, established certain rules for the perpetual direction of that motion; so, when he created man, and endued him with freewill to conduct himself in all parts of life, he laid down certain immutable laws of human nature, whereby that freewill is in some degree regulated and restrained, and gave him also the faculty of reason to discover the purport of those laws.

Considering the creator only as a being of infinite *power*, he was able unquestionably to have prescribed whatever laws he pleased to his creature, man, however unjust or severe. But as he is also a being of infinite *wisdom*, he has laid down only such laws as were founded in those relations of justice, that existed in the nature of things antecedent to any positive precept. These are the eternal, immutable laws of good and evil, to which the creator himself in all his dispensations conforms; and which he has enabled human reason to discover, so far as they are necessary for the conduct of human actions. Such among others are these principles: that we should live honestly, should hurt nobody, and should render to every one his due; to which three general precepts Justinian has reduced the whole doctrine of law. . . .

This law of nature, being coeval with mankind and dictated by God himself, is of course superior in obligation to any other. It is binding over all the globe in all countries, and at all times: no human laws are of any validity, if contrary to this; and such of them as are valid derive all their force, and all their authority, mediately or immediately, from this original.

While the colonists could not possibly have accepted Blackstone's assertion of parliamentary supremacy, they found his definition of natural law too satisfying to ignore. Indeed, they were delighted to quote a famous Tory for their purposes.

The law of nature, whatever its source and however

defined, had at least four basic applications or meanings in Revolutionary political thought. First, it was a set of moral standards governing private conduct. There were, it was generally believed, certain rules of human behavior discoverable through reason, experience, or revelation. Justinian had reduced these "immutable laws of good and evil" to three blunt commands; Americans reduced them further to one: the Golden Rule. According to Spartanus in the *New-Hampshire Gazette*:

For the greatest of all laws that respect mankind, is, to love our neighbours as ourselves, and do as we would be done by.

Prosperity and happiness were the lot of men who obeyed this law, adversity and sadness the lot of men who did not. Since the good state (the state shaped to the laws of nature) rested on good men (men who obeyed the laws of nature), one of the duties of the political community was to encourage virtue and discourage vice. The cult of virtue, of which we shall learn in Chapter 13, was an intimate corollary of natural law. The virtuous life was the natural life, just as good government was natural government.

Next, the laws of nature formed a system of abstract justice to which the laws of men should conform. Positive law that ran counter to a community's inherited sense of right and wrong was not only bad law but no law at all, for had not Blackstone himself asserted that "no human laws are of any validity if contrary to . . . the law of nature"? The chief business of an assembly was therefore to search proposed legislation for clauses or commands that outraged accepted notions of abstract justice. A law was a good law and demanded obedience,

James Wilson wrote, if it was "founded on the law of nature." The British Constitution was the greatest of all systems of government, Lord Camden observed, because it was "grounded on the eternal and immutable laws of nature."

But the law of nature, at least in American opinion, was something more than a model of perfection to which positive law should conform. It was also a line of demarcation around the proper sphere of political authority. Governments that pushed beyond it did so at peril of resistance or even revolution. Since the greatest and freest of constitutions was an earthly replica of natural law, any violation of it was both unconstitutional and unnatural. The Massachusetts House of Representatives told the other assemblies "that in all free States the Constitution is fixed; & as the supreme Legislative derives its Power & Authority from the Constitution, it cannot overleap the Bounds of it without destroying its own Foundation." This, of course, was Locke's great message: that government must respect the commands of natural law or release men from obedience. In time Americans came to regard natural law as the one clear restriction on Parliament's power to tax or govern the colonies. Since it was "repugnant to the Laws of Nature," Edward Bancroft announced, "for the Subjects of one State to exercise Jurisdiction over those of another," the people of the second state, in this instance the immediate guardians of those laws, must apply whatever sanctions they had at their command.

Finally and most important, natural law was the source of natural rights. A truly free people, Jefferson wrote, would claim "their rights as derived from the laws of nature, and not as the gift of their chief magistrate" or of the community. Thus it became necessary to establish the existence of natural law in order to provide an unbreachable defense for the rights of man. In the final reckoning, natural law came to be equated with natural rights. Most colonists were so intent upon proving that this law was the one great source and defense of their rights that they used these expressions interchangeably.

In basing their final campaign of resistance to imperial power on "the supreme and uncontrollable laws of nature," the American colonists stood firm in one of their greatest traditions. The higher law, whether proceeding from God or nature or history, had been part of men's thinking since the first settlements. By the time of the Revolution it was a universally accepted article of faith. If hundreds of New England preachers could declaim upon the law of nature, certainly their leading seminary of learning could make General Washington in 1776 a "Doctor of Laws, the Law of Nature and Nations, and the Civil Law." If a philosopher could invoke "the Laws of Nature and of Nature's God" in behalf of a whole people, certainly one of the least of this people, a runaway servant crying for help in the *Pennsylvania Packet* in 1771, could invoke them for release from his contract. Bentham might blast natural law as "nothing but a phrase . . . the natural tendency of [which] is to compel a man by the force of conscience, to rise up in arms against any law whatever that he happens not to like"; Americans seemed not the least bit bothered by its inherent inconsistencies and dangers. The mind of God as read by revelation, the plan of nature as analyzed by right reason, and the history of mankind as interpreted by the scholars of the nation all proclaimed the reality of moral limits on political power. If the rest of the world could not agree that certain truths were self-evident, then the rest of the world was simply ignoring the plain dictates of universal justice.

SEVEN

Man: His
Nature and His Rights

THE CONTRASTING PHILOSOPHIES of Hobbes and Locke, or of Calhoun and Jefferson, make clear that any particular system of political theory is a reflection of the opinion held by its author about the nature of man. Certainly this was true of American political thought in the Revolutionary period. Indeed, thinkers and debaters devoted special attention to this question. Their sermons and pamphlets are full of assumptions and comments about the natural virtues and vices of the men about them. They were bothered not at all by a lack of scientific psychological data; the lessons of history, properly selected, gave support to all possible shadings of opinion.

The American consensus dictated no particular estimate of the nature of man. Patriot philosophers with identical opinions about the location of sovereignty could entertain the most divergent views about the reasoning powers of men, and a single thinker might ad-

vance two or three different estimates within the pages
of one tract. A good deal depended, of course, upon the
author's immediate purpose. An argument for home rule
would lead him to sweeping generalizations about self-
reliance and sociability. A tirade against the British ministry would evoke equally broad comments about man's
vicious nature. We must remember that the colonists
were heirs of several great and cross-cutting traditions.
A son of the Puritans who was also a child of the Enlightenment could be indulged a little confusion on this
crucial point.

We may reduce the wide range of opinion on the
nature of man to three general attitudes. One small
group of thinkers, of whom Jefferson was perhaps the
boldest, took the "enlightened" view, considering man a
naturally good, decent, friendly, capable person whose
troubles were the bitter fruit of a world he had never
made. Another, to which many Calvinist preachers belonged, clung to doctrines of sin and depravity, prefer-
ring to lay stress, as did John Witherspoon, on "the ignorance, prejudice, partiality and injustice of human
nature." Most thinkers settled down between these two
extremes, finding much that was good and much that
was bad in the character of every single man. Said the
author of a piece entitled "Loose thoughts on GOVERN-
MENT" in the *Virginia Gazette* in 1776:

In whatever situation we take a view of man, whether
ranging the forests in the rude state of his primeval existence,
or in the smooth situation of polished society; wheresoever
we place him, on the burning sands of Africa, the freezing
coasts of Labrador, or the more congenial climes of the tem-
perate zones, we shall every where find him the same complex

being, a slave to his passions, and tossed and agitated by a thousand disagreeing virtues and discordant vices.

What exactly were those fundamental traits that Revolutionary thinkers found ingrained in man? Which ones were most significant for political organization?

Four qualities that our culture considers "good" were given special stress in the literature of the Revolution: *sociability*, the impulse to associate and co-operate with other men in pursuit of common ends; *love of liberty*, which makes it unnatural and therefore impossible for a man to submit to slavery; *goodness*, the quality of basic human decency that inspires every man, in the words of John Adams, to "a love of truth, and a veneration for virtue"; and *rationality*, the ability to read, understand, and apply "the eternal laws of natural justice, humanity and equity." Five qualities that we would consider "bad" were stressed with equal vigor, as often as not by the same authors who extolled man's goodness: *selfishness*, the impulse to seek one's own happiness even in defiance of the common good; *depravity*, the quality of sinfulness —of jealousy, injustice, anger, ignorance, deceit, vanity, and intemperance—that lurks in every human soul; *passion*, the refusal to be rational, which Rev. Phillips Payson found to be "as natural to men as reason" itself; *moral laziness*, "Inattention to the real Importance of things," which brings men to slavery contrary to nature and their wills; and *corruptibility*, the inevitable result of "the passion for acquiring power" which operates so "forcibly on the human mind." All these "disagreeing virtues and discordant vices" were thought to be present to some degree in every man, no matter how lofty his station or low his character.

Perhaps the most politically significant of all these qualities was sociability, the urge man feels to associate with other men, even if this means surrendering a substantial part of his original freedom. So pointed was the emphasis placed upon "the social Principle in man" that many thinkers excluded the pre-social state of nature, and therefore natural man, from serious consideration. Man was clearly a social animal, Joseph Warren observed, a being "formed for social life." If he had a natural state, that state was society, James Otis agreed, for " 'tis clear that men cannot live apart or independent of each other." Society itself was therefore natural, and few men if any could be said to be in it by free choice. While American thinkers were understandably confused in this matter, it seems clear that the most thoughtful of them made a distinction between society and government. The former was the "natural" result of the presence of a number of men in a certain area; the latter was the mechanistic if inevitable result of an act of will. In short, the contract in Revolutionary thought was governmental, not social.

The one other quality deserving special mention was the transformation that is more than likely to come over man when he is placed in a situation of power. Revolutionary thinkers, beset by threats of arbitrary British policy, generally agreed with Hamilton that "a fondness for power is implanted in most men, and it is natural to abuse it when acquired." "The history of mankind," James Iredell wrote, "unhappily justifies the strongest suspicion of men in authority." "Every man by nature," Rev. Thomas Allen of Pittsfield echoed, "has the seeds of tyranny deeply implanted within him." Although this belief in man's love of power was not nearly so strong or widely advertised as it was later to be in Federalist political thought, few authors failed to mention it as a human characteristic, and none went out of his way to deny it specifically. The universal American belief in constitutionalism and the rule of law—indeed in the necessity of a written, comprehensible constitution —derived from this suspicious appraisal of man in authority. No one ever spoke more succinctly to this point than Samuel Adams:

All men are fond of Power. It is difficult for us to be prevaild upon to believe that we possess more than belongs to us. Even publick Bodies of men legally constituted are too prone to covet more Power than the Publick hath judgd it safe to entrust them with. It is happy when their Power is not only subject to Controul while it is exercisd, but frequently reverts into the hands of the People from whom it is derived, and to whom Men in Power ought for ever to be accountable.

If man was a composite of good and evil, of ennobling excellencies and degrading imperfections, then one of the chief ends of the community, an anonymous Virginian advised, was "to separate his virtues from his vices," to help him purposefully to pursue his better nature. The achievement of this purpose called for two types of collective action: establishing or encouraging institutions, especially religious and political institutions, that would give free play to his virtues while controlling or suppressing his vices; educating him to recognize the sweet harvest of the one and bitter fruits of the other. True religion encouraged man to suppress his savage impulses; constitutional government forced him to think before acting; sound education taught him the delights of virtue and liberty.

Whatever disagreement might have existed over man's other natural or social characteristics, all American thinkers conceded him a capacity for learning. Different men could acquire knowledge in different amounts, but all men could acquire the minimum necessary for survival and citizenship. Man was something more than a fortuitous complex of virtues and vices. He was *educable* —he could learn and be taught. More to the point, he could learn why to cherish virtue and shun vice, how to serve the community and defend liberty. Free government rested on virtue, virtue on knowledge, knowledge on regular techniques of education. It was therefore the business of government, Rev. Simeon Howard pointed out in 1780, "to make provision for schools and all suitable means of instruction." The exigencies of the economy, the weight of tradition, and the unsettled state of the times conspired against general acceptance of the doctrine of free and universal public education, yet no political thinker doubted the imperative necessity of community action in this crucial area. The eloquent words of Rev. Phillips Payson expressed American thinking about education for liberty in the darkest year of the struggle, 1778:

The slavery of a people is generally founded in ignorance of some kind or another; and there are not wanting such facts as abundantly prove the human mind may be so sunk and debased, through ignorance and its natural effects, as even to adore its enslaver, and kiss its chains. Hence knowledge and learning may well be considered as most essentially requisite to a free, righteous government. . . .

Every kind of useful knowledge will be carefully encouraged and promoted by the rulers of a free state. . . . The education of youth, by instructors properly qualified, the establishment of societies for useful arts and sciences, the encouragement of persons of superior abilities, will always command the attention of wise rulers.

Political thinkers naturally emphasized the acquisition of political knowledge. Said John Jay on the inauguration of the New York Constitution of 1777:

Let virtue, honor, the love of liberty and of science be, and remain, the soul of this constitution, and it will become the source of great and extensive happiness to this and future generations. Vice, ignorance, and want of vigilance, will be the only enemies able to destroy it. Against these provide, and, of these, be forever jealous. Every member of the state, ought diligently to read and study the constitution of his country, and teach the rising generation to be free. By knowing their rights, they will sooner perceive when they are violated, and be the better prepared to defend and assert them.

Others called attention to the mutual dependence of liberty and learning. Education and knowledge were as much the effect as the cause of free government. The infant republic could look forward confidently to intellectual splendor. Dr. David Ramsay was one of many who prophesied:

Every circumstance concurs to make it probable, that the arts and sciences will be cultivated, extended, and improved, in independent America. . . . Our free governments are the proper nurseries of rhetoric, criticism, and the arts which are founded on the philosophy of the human mind. In monarchies, an extreme degree of politeness disguises the simplicity of nature, and "sets the looks at variance with the thoughts"; in republics, mankind appear as they really are, without any false coloring: In these governments, therefore, attentive observers have an opportunity of knowing all the avenues to the heart, and of thoroughly understanding human nature. The great inferiority of the moderns to the ancients in fine writing, is to be referred to this veil cast over mankind by the artificial refinements of modern monarchies. From the operation of similar causes, it is hoped, that the free governments of America will produce poets, orators, critics and historians, equal to the most celebrated of the ancient commonwealths of Greece and Italy.

While many Americans may have smiled at the grandeur of this hope, few doubted the capacity of "this numerous, brave and hardy people" to learn the rights and duties of citizenship in a free republic. No characteristic of man had more political significance than his innate capacity for instruction in virtue and freedom.

The natural character of man was an alloy of virtue and vice; his natural state was pure freedom and equality. "All men are, by nature, equal and free," James Wilson wrote; "no one has a right to any authority over another without his consent." Revolutionary thinkers were in virtually unanimous accord on this point. Men might be grossly unequal in appearance, talents, intelligence, virtue, and fortune, but to this extent at least they were absolutely equal: No man had any natural right of dominion over any other; every man was free in the sight of God and plan of nature. The ranks and privileges of organized society were the result of unnatural usurpation, faulty institutions, the dead hand of an ignorant past, or the inevitable division of men into rulers and ruled.

The principle of natural equality was not incompatible with political, social, or economic stratification, but the burden of proof was squarely on advocates of artificial inequality. It was for them to demonstrate that an unequal arrangement was essential to the stability, prosperity, or independence of the community. Conversely, the goal of political science was to discover a political pattern that would recreate the equality of rights and near-equality of property that had preceded the formation of government. The glory of a free constitution, John Adams pointed out, was that it reduced these social inequalities to the barest minimum and preserved as much natural equality "as is compatible with the people's security against foreign invasion and domestic usurpation."

It is important to note these two aspects of the doctrine of natural equality to which most Revolutionists subscribed: that equality among men existed within a limited sphere, but that within this sphere all men were created absolutely equal. Each had an equal claim to be free of any earthly power; each could be governed only with his consent. In this sense equality was both an essential feature of human relations and an essential principle of libertarian political thought. It was an article of faith, a challenge to constitution-makers, and the central arrangement of political organization. James Otis was not really joking when he wrote in support of natural equality:

No government has a right to make hobby horses, asses and slaves of the subject, nature having made sufficient of the two former, for all the lawful purposes of man, from the harmless peasant in the field, to the most refined politician in the cabinet; but none of the last, which infallibly proves they are unnecessary.

No system of political thought, however detached or speculative, ever ranges in perfect symmetry over all great questions of power, organization, and obedience. The political thinker concentrates inevitably upon the problems of his own civilization. His theoretical structure is proportioned to "the felt necessities" of the age rather than to a standard, timeless pattern in which every possible question receives its just due. The men of the Revolution were no exception to this rule. Heirs of a great tradition of personal liberty, children of an age concerned with the individual rather than the community, targets of a policy that seemed to defy the dictates of abstract justice, they used up most of their energy defining the rights of man and devising methods of protecting them. They were individualists because the individual was under fire, limitationists because a government had overleaped its limits, constitutionalists because the existence of their constitution hung in the balance. Above all, they were exponents of natural rights. A legislature claiming the power to bind them in all cases whatsoever had moved decisively against their liberty and property, and they meant to stand and fight this invasion on the broadest possible ground.

The doctrine of natural rights was therefore the hard core of Revolutionary political thought; the possession of natural rights was the essence of being human. Like almost all other exponents of higher law, Americans gave this law a content and meaning that suited their practical purpose. The natural rights of man were so useful, even essential, to this purpose that they were willing to equate them with natural law itself. The rights of man, that is to say, not only depended upon or sprang from natural law; they *were* natural law, at least so far as it could be

understood by men. In the political thought of the
American Revolution natural law was all but swallowed
up in natural rights. The dictates, indeed the content, of
"the supreme and uncontrollable laws of nature" became
"the *absolute* rights of individuals." If a man wished to
follow the path of universal justice, he had only to understand and respect these rights. In our effort to understand the doctrine of natural rights as expounded in the
Revolutionary period we must seek answers to these questions: What exactly was meant by the phrase "natural
rights"? What was the source of these rights? What specific rights of man were covered by this concept?

By natural rights the Revolutionists meant simply
those rights which belong to man as man. They used
several adjectives in addition to "natural" to express the
special quality of these rights. They were *natural,* traceable directly to the great plan of nature if not indeed
derived from "the great Legislator of the universe"; *absolute,* belonging to man before, outside of, and quite without regard to organized government or society; *eternal,*
never varying in content or identity; *essential,* since necessary to man's existence as man; and *unalienable* (or inalienable), "of that importance, that no equivalent can
be received in exchange." Inherent, universal, unalterable, inestimable, sacred, indefeasible, fundamental, im-
prescriptible, divine, God-given, hereditary, and indeli-
ble were other adjectives used to stamp the natural rights
of mankind with transcendent significance. In the heat
of the struggle over the authority of Parliament, some
American authors carelessly or designedly confused natural rights with civil or constitutional rights. But more
serious thinkers like Otis, Hamilton, and Parsons expressed the true sense of the patriot school when they

distinguished those rights which were natural, absolute, eternal, essential, and unalienable from those which were constitutional, civil, social, or relative.

The fact or fiction of the state of nature was especially serviceable in clearing up this confusion. In the last analysis, natural rights were different from civil or constitutional rights because they had belonged to man in the state of nature. He had brought them with him into society; he had brought them with him into government. And he would take them with him should he ever return to the state of nature or of natural society. In any case, a fundamental article of the American faith was the belief that every man—no matter what his station, calling, learning, and fortune—had certain natural, unalienable rights. These were, John Adams insisted, "antecedent to all earthly government," incapable of being surrendered to government, and identified with nature or with God himself. Perhaps most important to patriot purposes, they served as the ultimate standard for human laws and the ultimate check upon arbitrary power.

The sources of natural rights were the sources of natural law: God, nature, history. For the most part colonial thinkers were willing to merge God and nature into one magnificent and consecrated source. An occasional author, especially if he occupied a dissenting pulpit, might speak specifically, as did Rev. Stephen Johnson, of "natural liberty" as "a gift of the beneficent Creator to the whole human race," but most would have agreed with John Dickinson's message to the Committee of Correspondence in Barbados:

Kings or parliaments could not *give* the *rights essential to happiness,* as you confess those invaded by the Stamp Act to be. We claim them from a higher source—from the King of kings, and Lord of all the earth. They are not annexed to us by parchments and seals. They are created in us by the decrees of Providence, which establish the laws of our nature. They are born with us; exist with us; and cannot be taken from us by any human power, without taking our lives. In short, they are founded on the immutable maxims of reason and justice.

Men like Hamilton and Jefferson might have wished to ignore or at least neutralize the hand of God, but they, like Dickinson, were always careful to mention both God and nature. No passage in Revolutionary literature is more justly famous than Hamilton's flamboyant escape from the trap of the Tory argument that New York had no charter and New Yorkers therefore no charter rights:

The Sacred Rights of Mankind are not to be rummaged for among old parchments or musty records. They are written, as with a sunbeam, in the whole volume of human nature, by the Hand of the Divinity itself, and can never be erased or obscured by mortal power.

A few writers described the rights of man as "hard-earned." John Adams in particular went deep into the past to remind his readers that these rights, although traceable to God and nature, had in fact been secured in laws and constitutions only after bitter struggles against despotism and indifference. He who wished to identify those rights which no government should touch must look not only to "the nature of man" but to "the history of nations." Throughout the political thinking of this history-conscious people runs this implicit assumption: Natural and unalienable rights are those basic liberties which are enjoyed and respected wherever men are free, prosperous, and happy. Washington was thinking of rights as the legacy of history rather than the gift of God when he wrote the state governors in 1783:

The foundation of our empire was not laid in the gloomy age of ignorance and superstition; but at an epocha when the rights of mankind were better understood and more clearly defined, than at any former period. The researches of the human mind after social happiness have been carried to a great extent; the treasures of knowledge, acquired by the labors of philosophers, sages, and legislators, through a long succession of years, are laid open for our use, and their collective wisdom may be happily applied in the establishment of our forms of government.

What were these rights which man possessed as man and could never surrender? In the pamphlets, sermons, and documents of the Revolution almost every conceivable human right—including the right to brew beer at home—was proclaimed to be natural, unalienable, and essential to the good society. But in works that were more political philosophy than propaganda we find these rights singled out as the legitimate possession of all men everywhere: life, liberty, property, conscience, and happiness.

The right to life was so far above dispute that authors were content merely to mention it in passing. Blackstone had not been able to say much more than that it was "the immediate gift of God, a right inherent by nature in every individual," and no American was going to improve on that celebrated man of the law. The strategic importance of the right to life lay in its great corollary or defense: the law or right of self-preservation. This secondary right made it possible for a single man or a whole nation to meet force with force, to resist arbitrary invasions of life, liberty, and property.

The natural right to liberty was central to all other rights, and the literature of the Revolution is full of salutes to its blessings and excellencies. "Liberty!" had been the American watchword for so many generations that no author, Whig or Tory, ever doubted in print that it was, as James Iredell wrote, "in some degree . . . the right of every human creature." Indeed, man without natural liberty was a contradiction in terms. "The god who gave us life," Jefferson wrote to George III, "gave us liberty at the same time." Liberty was defined simply as the freedom and power of each individual to act as he pleased "without restraint or control." From this natural liberty, the freedom from "obligation to obedience," flowed all other liberties that men enjoyed in society.

Americans, of course, were concerned about specific liberties in the political community rather than the original liberty of man in the state of nature. Most of their discussions of liberty are therefore somewhat confused. Yet we can discover certain common ideas about natural liberty in even the most occasional apostrophes. A good example of the way in which the colonial thinker dealt with liberty is a communication of 1765 to the *New-York Gazette*:

Liberty, as it is the honour and glory of a nation, so also it is their pleasure and happiness. There is not perhaps one temporal blessing bestowed by the supreme being on mankind that is more agreeable when enjoyed; more difficult to be parted with; or more desirable when absent. A love for Liberty seems interwoven with our very nature; and we are always ready to pronounce a people happy or miserable in proportion as they are possessed or destitute of it. . . .

There is perhaps nothing in this life more essential to our happiness. It is the state for which we are naturally calculated. It is what we all desire. The absence of it produces positive pain, as well as the presence of it positive happiness. It is the fountain of wealth, and of all real honours. For I cannot conceive of any true dignity a Slave can enjoy; for although he commands a thousand or ten thousand others, he is yet but a Slave himself.

Colonial thinkers, even the holders of slaves, concurred generally with this author's assumption that all men were naturally free. Most arguments for abolition of Negro slavery advanced in the Revolution were based on the doctrine of natural, unalienable liberty.

Perhaps the most interesting subsidiary right that Revolutionary pamphleteers deduced from natural liberty was, in the words of Jefferson,

a right, which nature has given to all men, of departing from the country in which chance, not choice has placed them, of going in quest of new habitations, and of there establishing new societies, under such laws and regulations as to them shall seem most likely to promote public happiness.

The natural right of migration was extremely useful to the cause, since it permitted Americans to argue that their ancestors had left England as free agents and had made a fresh contract with the sovereign left behind. Richard Bland and Jefferson were the two most vocal exponents of this radical doctrine, and each made clear that "the natural right of an individual to remove his person and effects wherever he pleases" was a direct corollary of the essential freedom stamped indelibly on man's nature. The hardy migrants of Vermont placed this statement in their first Declaration of Rights:

All people have a natural and inherent right to emigrate from one State to another, that will receive them; or to form a new State in vacant countries, or in such countries as they can purchase, whenever they think that thereby they can promote their own happiness.

The right to acquire and enjoy property was universally acclaimed in the literature of the Revolution. "The law of nature," wrote someone masquerading as Sidney in the Norfolk *Virginia Gazette,* "being founded in reason and justice admits of property." Samuel Adams spoke for all American publicists when he told General Conway, "It is acknowledged to be an unalterable law in nature, that a man should have the free use and sole disposal of the fruit of his honest industry, subject to no controul." And elsewhere he announced:

It is observable, that though many have disregarded life, and contemned liberty, yet there are few men who do not agree that property is a valuable acquisition, which ought to be held sacred. Many have fought, and bled, and died for this, who have been insensible to all other obligations. Those who ridicule the ideas of right and justice, faith and truth among men, will put a high value upon money. Property is admitted to have an existence, even in the savage state of nature. The bow, the arrow, and the tomahawk; the hunting and the fishing ground, are species of property, as important to an American savage, as pearls, rubies, and diamonds are to the Mogul, or a Nabob in the East, or the lands, tenements, hereditaments, messuages, gold and silver of the Europeans. And if property is necessary for the support of savage life, it is by no means less so in civil society.

Although Locke had several times used the word "property" in the broad sense of everything a man is or has,

Americans usually limited their definition to ownership of things tangible or at least convertible to money. Property in this sense was so essential to the fulfillment of man's promise and powers that it could almost be equated with liberty itself. If Locke included liberty in his definition of property, colonists included property in their definition of liberty. As one anonymous contributor put the matter in the *Boston Gazette* (or, as Tories labeled it, "The Weekly Dung-Barge"), "*Liberty* and *Property* are not only join'd in common discourse, but are in their own natures so nearly ally'd that we cannot be said to possess the one without the enjoyment of the other." This was not because Americans were more materialistic than other people. Quite the contrary, their primary concern was with the political and spiritual aspects of human freedom. But the crisis of the moment, to which their thoughts were directed, was an unprecedented invasion of the right to dispose of property without compulsion: that is, the right of men to be taxed only by representatives of their own choosing. The men of the Revolution were no more obsessed than their ancestors or descendants with what Richard Henry Lee acclaimed as the great right of "virtuous enjoyment and free possession of property honestly gained." Few thinkers ever doubted, however, that it was a natural right of man, and not a right granted by society. The town of Newburyport spoke for all America when it lectured its representative to the General Assembly in 1765:

That a People should be taxed at the Will of another, whether of one Man or many, without their own Consent in Person or by Representative, is *rank* Slavery. For if their Superior sees fit, they may be deprived of their whole Property, upon any frivolous Pretext, or without any Pretext at all.

And a People, without Property, or in the precarious Possession of it, are in no better State than Slaves; for Liberty, or even Life itself, without the Enjoyment of them flowing from Property, are of no Value.

Only two other rights—the right of conscience and the right to happiness—were ever placed by more than one or two authors at the same level of sanctity and universality with life, liberty, and property. In one sense, of course, each of these rights was simply a derivative of natural liberty. Yet, in another and more important sense, they were considered to have an existence of their own. Each was essential to the full expression of man's inherent nature; each was plainly antecedent to society and government. The right to happiness—or at least to pursue happiness without interference—was a logical assumption in the political thought of men to whom rationalism had made a powerful appeal. Happiness rather than salvation seemed now to be man's chief obsession. Through all the writings of men like Wilson, R. H. Lee, Jefferson, Iredell, and Mayhew runs a firm belief that "the Creator surely wills the happiness of his Creatures," that God, in Iredell's view, "did not make men to be unhappy,"

that mankind were intended to be happy, at least that God gave them the power of being so, if they would properly exert the means He has bestowed upon them.

Or as John Dickinson put it:

It would be an insult on the divine Majesty to say, that he has given or allowed any man or body of men *a right to make me miserable*. If no man or body of men has *such a right*, I have a *right to be happy*. If there can be no happiness without freedom, I have a *right to be free*.

Jefferson was more than a felicitous penman when he proclaimed the "pursuit of happiness" to be a natural right of man, for by the time of the Declaration most thinkers agreed with him on this point. He was, however, something of a nonconformist in substituting this right for that of property. He alone seems to have flirted seriously with the advanced view that property was a social rather than natural right.

The right of conscience, the right of each individual to reach out for God without interference or even assistance from other men, was naturally of prime interest to a people well on the way to full religious liberty. William Livingston reminded his fellow countrymen in these angry words that political interference with a man's religious opinions was a violation of the commands of natural justice:

Who, in a state of nature, ever deemed it an inconvenience that every man should choose his own religion? Did the free denizens of the world . . . ever worry one another for not practising ridiculous rites, or for believing things incredible? Did men in their aboriginal condition ever suffer persecution for conscience sake? The most frantic enthusiast will not pretend it. Why then should the members of society be supposed, on their entering into it, to have had in contemplation the reforming an abuse which never existed?

While the men of the Revolution may have been given to fantastic hyperbole and astounding ambiguity in discussing rights and privileges, we must have no doubt of their sincerity and conviction in placing special value on these five rights: life, liberty, property, happiness, and conscience.

EIGHT

The Rights of Americans

IF THE FIVE NATURAL rights belonged to man as man—to man, that is to say, in a real or conjectured state of nature —what happened after the formation of government? What rights could a man properly claim as a member of a free community? More concretely, what rights could an American claim as a member of his free community? To answer these questions we must again quote a few famous words on the origin and purpose of government:

> We hold these truths to be self-evident, that all men are created equal, that they are endowed by their Creator with certain unalienable Rights, that among these are Life, Liberty, and the pursuit of Happiness. That to secure these rights, Governments are instituted among Men, deriving their just powers from the consent of the governed.

At this point Revolutionary thinkers ran full tilt into trouble. If the natural rights of man were really unalienable, how could a government be expected to secure them? In the act of escaping from the insecurities of the state of nature and entering an organized community, a man had to agree to certain restraints upon his original freedom. He could not possibly live in peace with his fellow men and retain the full measure of natural liberty. Yet how could he alienate that which was unalienable?

While most authors went blithely ahead in ignorance or disdain of this difficult question, the best of them would have agreed to two correlative distinctions worked out by Theophilus Parsons: one between "the surrendering of a power to controul our natural rights" and the surrendering of the rights themselves, the other between rights alienable and rights unalienable in the former and more limited sense of alienation of control. According to Parsons, only one natural right—the right of conscience —is completely unalienable: A man can surrender neither the right itself nor his original power to control it. The power to control the other natural rights, however, can be surrendered by a freely contracting individual— in return for a proper equivalent. "In a state of nature," Parsons explained,

every man had the sovereign controul over his own person. He might also have, in that state, a qualified property. . . . Over this qualified property every man in a state of nature had also a sovereign controul. And in entering into political society, he surrendered this right of controul over his person and property, (with an exception to the rights of conscience) to the supreme legislative power, to be exercised by that power, *when the good of the whole demanded it.* This was all the right he could surrender, being all the alienable right of which he was possessed. The only objects of legislation therefore, are the person and property of the individuals which compose the state.

In the words of another thinker, who chose a Tory paper, *Rivington's New-York Gazetteer* (1773), as his arena of disputation:

Men in a state of nature were equal. Their actions were subject to no limitations but those which arose from the laws of God. But through want of a common judge finally to determine their respective rights, and power sufficient to vindicate them, injuries must often have remained unredressed, or been punished by private revenge, beyond the demand of justice. *Civil Society* remedies these evils, adjusting the rights of individuals by a common wisdom, and protecting the exercise of them by a common power. It restricts every man from acting in such a manner as to injure others, as it restrains others from injuring him.

In short, men can surrender to the political community a certain amount of the original power to control their persons and properties. Just how much of this power they can and should surrender is a key question of political theory, to be answered in each instance according to the circumstances of the society and characters of the men who make it up. Every man must surrender enough control over his original liberty to permit government to maintain an organized, stable, peaceful pattern of human relations; no man should surrender so much that government dictates his every action. Between these two self-evident extremes the balance of liberty and authority must ever be in constant motion. The benefit of the doubt should be extended to liberty rather than authority. As a home-grown political thinker observed in the *Norwich Packet* in 1775:

There is no doubt, but by entering into society, mankind voluntarily give up a part of their natural rights, and bind themselves to the obedience of laws, calculated for the general good. But, we must distinguish between authority and oppression; between laws and capricious dictates; and keeping the original intention of government ever in view, we should take care that no more restraint be laid upon natural liberty, than what the necessities of society require.

It is the business of lawgivers and political scientists to search in good faith for the delicate balance between liberty and authority, between the desire and duty of the individual to retain as much control as possible over his person and property and the responsibility of government to maintain peace and order by "restrict[ing] every man from acting in such a manner as to injure others." In a free state the balance tips decisively in the direction of liberty. Men in such a state are generally virtuous; they make a conscious effort to use their freedom and property in a way that does not interfere with the freedom and property of men with whom they must live and do business. Government intervention is the exception rather than the rule. In autocratic states, where men are usually ignorant and immoral, the balance tips just as decisively toward authority. Government is arbitrary because men will not respect one another. The limits between liberty and political power in any particular community are set by the general state of morality, knowledge, and common agreement.

To this extent, then, American thinkers withdrew from the untenable position that natural rights were absolute and unalienable: A man can alienate part of the original power to control his rights. It is possible and proper for government to take his life, qualify his liberty, regulate his property, direct his search for happiness—even forbid all antisocial outward manifestations of the inner drives of conscience—if this is done in fulfillment of a contract and in pursuit of known laws. The constitution and laws of every free state must recognize and protect man's natural rights. Whatever restrictions government places upon the free exercise of these rights must result from his freely given consent. The liberty that man retains is then properly styled "civil" or, if clearly acknowledged in fundamental law, "constitutional." In Hamilton's words, which most American thinkers echoed, *"Civil liberty is only natural liberty, modified and secured by the sanctions of civil society."* In the process of being modified in order to be secured, natural liberty becomes civil and civil liberty becomes constitutional.

This would seem a convenient place to dispose briefly of religious liberty, the civil version of the natural right to conscience. Most American thinkers were in accord on these points: The right to conscience was absolutely unalienable, and government had no authority to enforce religious conformity. Government nevertheless did have authority to forbid and punish anti-social actions resulting from the pressures of a free conscience. Freedom of religion was a political freedom; political and religious liberty were, Hamilton reminded his audience, "linked together in one indissoluble bond." Few could agree on the exact measure of religious liberty that free men should enjoy under free government. While the day of persecution and forced conformity was over, the day of establishment and anti-Catholicism lingered on. Yet if Americans were not quite ready for complete disestablishment and liberty of conscience for all men, even "Papists," they had moved a long way, in doctrine as in fact, from the medieval union of church and state. The Virginia Declaration of Rights expressed the best sentiments of the time:

Religion, or the duty which we owe to our Creator, and the manner of discharging it, can be directed only by reason and conviction, not by force or violence; and therefore all men are equally entitled to the free exercise of religion, according

to the dictates of conscience; and it is the duty of all to practice Christian forbearance, love, and charity towards each
other.

In the state of nature all men possessed the five natural
rights in equal degree. What became of this original
equality in the process of transforming them from their
natural to their civil character? Revolutionary thinkers
were in almost complete agreement that the contract
could not alter the fact of natural equality to life, liberty
(defined as liberty of action), conscience, and the pursuit
of happiness. They were in less complete yet fairly general agreement that inequality was admissible in property
and political liberty. In other words, all persons under a
particular government had surrendered control of their
rights to life and liberty of action to the same degree, but
they had surrendered control of their rights to property
and political liberty in varying degrees. Legal inequalities
in property and political rights were, however, to be carefully restricted. They were permissible only if necessary
to the preservation of peace, order, and independence.
This formula, of course, left room for bitter disagreement
between proponents of property qualifications for political
activity and heralds of manhood suffrage. William Henry
Drayton of Charleston and the unknown author of the
New Hampshire tract *The People the Best Governors*
(1776) spoke much the same political language, yet their
comments on the right of plain people to govern themselves showed them to be poles apart on the question of
democracy. Drayton complained in 1769 that a faction in
Charleston had

consulted *De Arduis Reipublicae,* with Men who were never
in a Way to study, or to advise upon any Points, but Rules

how to cut up a *Beast in the Market* to the best advantage, to *cobble* an old Shoe in the neatest Manner, or to build a *necessary* House. Nature never intended that *such Men* should be *profound Politicians* or *able Statesmen*.

To the contrary, rejoined the New Hampshire radical:

God gave mankind freedom by nature, made every man equal to his neighbor, and has virtually enjoined them to govern themselves by their own laws. . . . The people best know their own wants and necessities, and therefore are best able to rule themselves. Tent-makers, cobblers, and common tradesmen composed the legislature at Athens.

American pamphleteers proclaimed at least seven other civil rights in addition to those believed to be natural and unalienable: the freedoms of speech, press, assembly, and petition; civil supremacy; representation and free elections; jury trial and its attendant safeguards. If these were not the inherent possession of all men everywhere, they were certainly the possession or aspiration of all men living under free government. The first four were not only individual rights but social necessities, conditions essential to the conduct of representative government. The last two, representation and jury trial, were not only rights but the means of defending all other rights. No man could consider himself truly free were his person and property subject to the control of a legislative or judicial organ in which he was not represented.

Freedom of Speech, Press, Assembly, and Petition. Colonial pamphleteers seemed more anxious to proclaim than to analyze these political freedoms. They all concurred on several decisive points about the content and significance of these freedoms: that they were closely, indeed inseparably, connected; that they were derived from the natural right to liberty; and that they were as essential to the operation of free government as to the happiness of free men. American thinking about each of these rights had a strong social rather than individualistic bias.

Freedom of speech was rarely discussed as an isolated phenomenon, and then only in a general and confused manner—as witness the musings of an unknown writer in the *Boston Gazette* in 1767:

> Man, in a state of nature, has undoubtedly a right to speak and act without controul. In a state of civil society, that right is limited by the law—Political liberty consists in a freedom of speech and action, so far as the laws of a community will permit, and no farther: all beyond is criminal, and tends to the destruction of Liberty itself.—That Society whose laws least restrain the words and actions of its members, is most free.—There is no nation on the earth, where freedom of speech is more extensive than among the English: This is what keeps the constitution in health and vigour, and is in a great measure the cause of our preservation as a free people: For should it ever be dangerous to exercise this privilege, it is easy to see, without the spirit of prophecy, slavery and bondage would soon be the portion of Britons.

The social value attached to this liberty is also revealed in a comment of Rev. Samuel Cooke's that "freedom of speech . . . is essential to a free constitution, and the ruler's surest guide."

Freedom of press, which as often as not was considered synonymous with the freedoms of speech, discussion, inquiry, thought, and communication, naturally received special attention in newspapers. For the most part, authors and editors placed emphasis on the social utility of this key political freedom. It was an "eminent instrument of promoting knowledge," "one grand means of promoting public virtue," and the "great palladium of the public liberty." The last of these functions, one editor pointed out, was perhaps the most important:

Without this check, we should be liable to oppression, whenever a tyrant was in power; nay, an ambitious designing ruler, I dare to say, fears more the correction of the Press, than any other controul whatever; and it is to the freedom with which the conduct of the Great is scanned in England, that we are principally indebted for our glorious constitution.

Letter after letter to and from colonial editors paid tribute to the restraints a free press imposed on dangerous extensions of arbitrary power. English reprints, accounts of the Zenger trial of 1735, and original pieces were all ammunition for colonial batteries that never wore out saluting freedom of press as "one of the principal handmaids of liberty." "However little some may think of common newspapers," a Virginian wrote, "to a wise man they appear the Ark of God for the safety of the people." Freedom of press was sorely tried in the harsh, confusing days following the passage of the Coercive Acts, and American thinkers did their sincere best to defend the central position they had assigned to this freedom in the pattern of constitutional government.

The lively concern of Revolutionary journalists for the freedom their elders had wrung from reluctant politicians produced at least two laughs worth recording for history. The editor of the *New-Hampshire Gazette* ended an especially eloquent salute to the advantages of a free press with this piece of practical advice:

The Conclusion of the whole is, That unless many of the Customers of this Paper make better Pay than they have for several Years past, they must be deprived of these Advantages; and therefore it is hoped a *Word to the Wise* will be sufficient to induce them thereto: And many Persons who have been a long Time in Arrears for Advertisements, are desired also to discharge the same.

And the printer of the Wilmington *North-Carolina Gazette* spoke for many another bedeviled editor when he told his public:

The Printer hereof cannot help observing to the Publick, that he is at present in a very disagreeable Situation. At the earnest Desire, or rather stern Command of the People, he has endeavoured, with great Difficulty, to carry on a News-Paper, well knowing, that that Province that is deprived of the Liberty of the Press, is deprived of one of the darling Privileges which they, as Englishmen, boast of.—The Consequence has been, that, for publishing a Letter from a Gentleman at Tarborough . . . he has been THREATENED with a Horse-Whipping;—and doubtless he would have run some such Hazard, had he refus'd inserting that very Letter —What Part is he now to act?—Continue to keep his Press open and free, and be in Danger of Corporal Punishment, or block it up, and run the Risque of having his Brains knocked out? Sad Alternative.

The allied rights of assembly and petition were proclaimed in hundreds of town and county resolutions. In 1774 the towns of Middlesex County, Massachusetts, acknowledged the importance of these rights in this representative statement:

Resolved, That every people have an absolute right of meeting together to consult upon common grievances, and to petition, remonstrate, and use every legal method for their removal.

Resolved, That the act which prohibits these constitutional meetings cuts away the scaffolding of English supremacy, and reduces us to a most abject state of vassalage and slavery.

The rights of assembly and petition were especially important for the conduct of representative government. These ancient liberties existed primarily for the health of the community rather than for the happiness of the individual.

Civil Supremacy: No Standing Armies. The problem of civil-military relations weighed heavily on the minds of the colonists. By 1765 their Whig heritage and their contacts with British troops had given rise to an almost doctrinaire tradition of civil supremacy. The events of the next decade, especially the Boston massacre, served only to harden the conviction of men like Samuel Cooke that "military aid has ever been deemed dangerous to a free civil state, and has often been used as an effectual engine to subvert it." Two of the most telling indictments in Jefferson's catalogue of kingly sins were: "He has kept among us, in times of peace, standing Armies without the Consent of our legislatures," and "He has affected to render the Military independent of and superior to the Civil power."

The Revolutionary tradition of civil supremacy, proclaimed most vocally by orators in and around Boston, found expression in three popular assumptions: the inherent danger of standing or "mercenary" armies, "a tremendous curse to a state" and "the scourge of mankind"; the effectiveness, even superiority, of the militia; and the necessity of tight civil—that is, *legislative*—control over all military personnel at all times. The popular American solution was to do away completely with the military profession and make every able-bodied man both citizen and soldier. A few authors were willing to concede that regular armies might be necessary in time of war when all other means had failed, but most men were prisoners of the Cincinnatus complex: No army of mercenaries could ever fight as bravely or successfully as a "well-regulated militia" defending hearth and home. These notions, which were to govern American military policy for generations after the Revolution, are given typical expression in these passages:

Samuel Adams to the *Boston Gazette* in 1768:

It is a very improbable supposition, that any people can long remain free, with a strong military power in the very heart of their country: Unless that military power is under the direction of the people, and even then it is dangerous.— History, both ancient and modern, affords many instances of the overthrow of states and kingdoms by the power of soldiers, who were rais'd and maintain'd at first, under the plausible pretence of defending those very liberties which they afterwards destroyed. Even where there is a necessity of the military power, within the land, which by the way but rarely happens, a wise and prudent people will always have a watchful & a jealous eye over it; for the maxims and rules of the army, are essentially different from the genius of a free people, and the laws of a free government.

Josiah Quincy, Jr., at the time of the Coercive Acts:

No free government was ever founded or ever preserved it's liberty without uniting the characters of citizen and soldier in those destined for defence of the state. The sword should never be in the hands of any, but those who have an interest in the safety of the community. . . . Such are a well regulated militia composed of the freeholders, citizen and husbandman, who take up arms to preserve their property as individuals, and their rights as freemen.

James Lovell, the "Massacre Orator" in 1771:

The true strength and safety of every commonwealth or limited monarchy, is the bravery of its freeholders, its militia. By brave militias they rise to grandeur; and they come to ruin by a mercenary army.

And finally, the Town of Boston to its representatives, May 10, 1773:

Standing armies have for ever made shipwreck of free states. . . . The militia of the colony are its natural and best defence; and it is an approved maxim in all well-policed states, that the sword should never be entrusted but to those who combat *pro aris et focis;* and whose interest it is to preserve the public peace.

No standing armies, a well-regulated militia, and unqualified legislative control—these were the essentials of the early American tradition of civil supremacy, a tradition as important for the defense of individual liberty as for the success of constitutional government. The free citizen of a free government had a manifest right to be protected against military power and supremacy. Yet this right carried with it a clearly defined duty: to serve in the militia, to combine the characters of citizen and soldier. On this point all colonists were agreed. Southerners might look askance at "the New-England levelling doctrine" of a citizen army "raised, *officered* and *conducted* by common consent," but they were no less dedicated to the belief that "the natural strength, and only security of a free government" was "a well regulated militia."

Representation and Jury Trial. In 1765 the Town of Boston informed its representatives in the General Court:

> The most essential Rights of British Subjects are those of being represented in the same Body which exercises the Power of levying Taxes upon them, & of having their Property tryed by Jurys: These are the very Pillars of the British Constitution founded in the Common Rights of Mankind.

Representation in the supreme lawmaking and taxing legislature and trial by one's "peers of the vicinage, according to the course of [the] law" were the two "main Pillars of the British Constitution." Indeed, since the Constitution was "founded in the Common Rights of Mankind," since "the Rights of Nature" were "happily interwoven" in its "ancient fabrick," these two great liberties or methods of defending liberty were properly the birthright of free men everywhere. In order to enjoy and defend their natural liberties a people did not have to adopt an exact imitation of the English legislative and judicial pattern, but the solid foundation of all free governments was some form of equal representation and impartial trial. Only through such instruments of popular control could the people consent to necessary restrictions on their liberty and property.

John Adams expressed the devotion of the colonists to these two major constitutional arrangements in a passage that must be quoted at length. In one of his celebrated letters of 1766 from "The Earl of Clarendon to William Pym," Adams pointed to the "grand division of constitutional powers . . . into those of legislation and those of execution." Having justified the immediate participation of the people in the legislative power, he went on to say:

This popular power, however, when the numbers grew large, became impracticable to be exercised by the universal and immediate suffrage of the people; and this impracticability has introduced from the feudal system an expedient which we call representation. This expedient is only an equivalent for the suffrage of the whole people in the common management of public concerns. It is in reality nothing more than this, the people choose attorneys to vote for them in the great council of the nation, reserving always the fundamentals of the government, reserving also a right to give their attorneys instructions how to vote, and a right at certain, stated intervals, of choosing a-new; discarding an old attorney, and choosing a wiser and better. And it is this reservation of fundamentals, of the right of giving instructions, and of new elections, which creates a popular check upon the whole government. . . .

The other grand division of power is that of execution. And here the king is, by the constitution, supreme executor of the laws, and is always present, in person or by his judges, in his courts, distributing justice among the people. But the executive branch of the constitution, as far as respects the administration of justice, has in it a mixture of popular power too. . . . The people choose a grand jury, to make inquiry and presentment of crimes. Twelve of these must agree in finding the bill. And the petit jury must try the same fact over again, and find the person guilty, before he can be punished. Innocence, therefore, is so well protected in this wise constitution, that no man can be punished till twenty-four of his neighbors have said upon oath that he is guilty. So it is also in the trial of causes between party and party. No man's property or liberty can be taken from him till twelve men in his neighborhood have said upon oath, that by laws of his own making it ought to be taken away, that is, that the facts are such as to fall within such laws. . . .

These two popular powers, therefore, are the heart and lungs, the mainspring and the centre wheel, and without them the body must die, the watch must run down, the government must become arbitrary. . . . In these two powers consist wholly the liberty and security of the people. They have no other fortification against wanton, cruel power; no other indemnification against being ridden like horses, fleeced like sheep, worked like cattle, and fed and clothed like swine and hounds; no other defence against fines, imprisonments, whipping-posts, gibbets, bastinadoes, and racks.

In this forceful passage Adams set down most of the significant American refinements of the rights of representation and jury trial. As to representation, these points of general accord among the colonists should be noted:

The business of the supreme legislature was to make laws, lay taxes, redress grievances, and, in the opinion of Sam Adams, interpose "in the mal conduct of the executive." No other instrument of government had the right or capacity to bind the people, since only through their representatives could they give consent to external control over their persons and properties. "The rights of a people to tax themselves, is essential to their liberties," a writer in the New London *Connecticut Gazette* proclaimed flatly in 1770. "To submit to taxes in any other way, is compleat slavery." Neither taxation nor legislation without representation was possible under free government. For this reason, the "right of Representation" was the basic right of political man, the right "on which all other rights essentially depend."

The people's chief defense against executive misconduct or usurpation was the legislature rather than the judiciary. Article V of the Maryland Declaration of Rights of 1776 announced:

> That the right in the people to participate in the Legislature is the best security of liberty, and the foundation of all free government.

For this reason in particular, the legislature was entitled to meet frequently and for extended periods. "The necessity and importance of a legislative in being," Samuel Adams wrote, should resolve all conflicts between legislature and executive in favor of the former, that is, "in favor of the people."

Representation should be "equal," that is, apportioned in such a way as to guard against giving "an undue influence to some parts of the community over others." In the words of Theophilus Parsons:

> The rights of representation should be so equally and impartially distributed, that the representatives should have the same views, and interests with the people at large. They should think, feel, and act like them, and in fine, should be an exact miniature of their constituents. They should be (if we may use the expression) the whole body politic, with all it's property, rights, and priviledges, reduced to a smaller scale, every part being diminished in just proportion.

And of John Adams:

> It [the representative assembly] should be in miniature an exact portrait of the people at large. It should think, feel, reason, and act like them. That it may be the interest of this assembly to do strict justice at all times, it should be an equal representation, or, in other words, equal interests among the people should have equal interests in it.

The frontier towns and counties made excellent use of the doctrine of equal representation in their fight for seats in the provincial legislature.

Representation should be direct and contractual, not indirect and virtual. Representatives should follow the wishes of their constituents so far as humanly possible; the latter should therefore give detailed and frequent instructions to the former. American theories of representation were not especially subtle. Burke's appeal of 1774 would have received even shorter shrift from the electors of Boston than it did from those of Bristol. Most colonial theorists agreed with The Censor of Philadelphia

that the right of instructing lies with the constituents, and them only; that the representatives are bound to regard them as the dictates of their masters, and not left at liberty to comply with or reject them, as they may think proper.

For this reason in particular, that it made a mockery of notions of instruction and accountability, virtual representation was anathema to American opinion.

The elections on which equal and faithful representation was based were to be free and frequent. Free elections, where "no bribery, corruption, or undue influence . . . have place," were in Wilson's words the "point of last consequence to all free governments." Only through an uncorrupted and unintimidated suffrage could a people elect a legislature dedicated to the common weal. In 1776 an anonymous Virginian attested the importance attached to free elections in these blunt words:

The freedom of election is necessary for the well-being of the Laws and the liberties of the state, which would otherwise fall a sacrifice to the altars of bribery and corruption, and party-Spirit. To this end, the representatives should be the unbiassed choice of the people, by ballot, in which no man should make interest, either directly or indirectly, for himself or his friend, under the penalty of a heavy fine, and an exclusion from the house of representatives for ever; for it is generally found, that the people will choose right, if left to themselves.

Frequent elections, which in fact and principle meant annual elections, were the one sure way to secure almost continuous accountability. Not only was a short term the best possible guarantee that the legislature would remain "in miniature an exact portrait of the people at large"; it was a major bulwark against abuse and usurpation of power. "Elections may be septennial or triennial," John Adams wrote to John Penn,

but, for my own part, I think they ought to be annual; *for there is not in all science a maxim more infallible than this, where annual elections end, there slavery begins.*

Concerning "that firmest Barrier of *English* Liberty, THE TRIAL BY JURIES," American authors had little to say of an analytical nature. Certainly no one ever questioned its justice and workability, and it is unusual to happen upon a writer who does not speak of "this inestimable jewel" in the most glowing terms. The right to jury trial was generally considered to cover all other procedural rights, including "that great bulwark and palladium of English liberty," habeas corpus.

It is difficult to exaggerate the esteem in which the colonists held the representative legislature and jury trial. The vehemence of their defense of these two bulwarks of freedom was, of course, a direct reaction to the ministry's assault upon them in the Sugar and Stamp Acts. Yet American devotion to these ancient techniques was more than just occasional. Few believed that the representative assembly and jury trial could ever be improved upon as instruments of popular control of government. John Adams spoke for almost every American when he exclaimed:

> What a fine reflection and consolation is it for a man, that he can be subjected to no laws which he does not make himself, or constitute some of his friends to make for him,—his father, brother, neighbor, friend, a man of his own rank, nearly of his own education, fortune, habits, passions, prejudices, one whose life and fortune and liberty are to be affected, like those of his constituents, by the laws he shall consent to for himself and them! What a satisfaction is it to reflect, that he can lie under the imputation of no guilt, be subjected to no punishment, lose none of his property, or the necessaries, conveniences, or ornaments of life, which indulgent Providence has showered around him, but by the judgment of his peers, his equals, his neighbors, men who know him and to whom he is known, who have no end to serve by punishing him, who wish to find him innocent, if charged with a crime, and are indifferent on which side the truth lies, if he disputes with his neighbor!

NINE

The Right of Resistance

UNDER NORMAL conditions of free society and constitutional government, representation and jury trial formed the last and firmest line of defense against arbitrary power. Political conditions in the years that led to 1776 were far from normal, however, and the practical-minded colonists shaped their theory to fit this imperative fact. Representation was no defense against a legislature in which they were represented only "virtually" or not at all; jury trial was no defense against an executive operating through courts of vice-admiralty. Led by their pamphleteers and prodded by their preachers, the colonists therefore went in search of an extraordinary line of defense, and they found it in the ancient right of resistance to tyranny. American writers disagreed sharply over certain practical applications of this right, but none ever doubted its certain existence. What John Adams derided as "the most mischievous of all doctrines, that of passive obedience and non-resistance," had no place at all in the American "party line." In the words of William Smith:

The doctrine of absolute *Non-resistance* has been fully exploded among every virtuous people. The freeborn soul revolts against it.

And of James Otis:

He that would palm the doctrine of unlimited passive obedience upon mankind—is not only a fool and a knave, but a rebel against common sense, as well as the laws of God, of Nature, and his Country.

And of Camillus in the *Pennsylvania Gazette* in 1775:

Those ornaments of human nature, *Locke, Sydney, Hoadley,* and many other illustrious names, have so refuted these absurd doctrines of passive obedience and non-resistance; and they are so repugnant to the common sense and happiness of mankind, that it would be an affront to the understandings of my countrymen to suppose they could now admit of serious argument.

Jonathan Boucher and his few colleagues in high Toryism never made so little sense to Americans as when they preached the gospel of unquestioning submission. The very definition of a Tory, according to a correspondent of the New Haven *Connecticut Journal*, was "a maintainer of the infernal doctrine of arbitrary power, and indefeasible right on the part of the sovereign, and of passive obedience and non resistance" on the part of the subject.

The essential conservatism of Revolutionary thinkers is most clearly revealed in their handling of the doctrine of resistance, a doctrine, men like Rev. John Lathrop were quick to point out, that was "far from being new." Spokesmen of a people who denied indignantly, in the gamy language of Arthur Lee, that they were "big with disaffection, disobedience, sedition and treason," the American pamphleteers were extremely guarded in their comments on this delicate subject. It is impossible to discover an important author who wrote in defense of the right of *revolution,* or who acclaimed *resistance* as anything but a necessary and unpleasant evil. The whole effort of American thinkers was directed to restricting and qualifying—one might say *legalizing*—the extraordinary right of appealing to arms.

One example of this conservative position was the insistence of most writers on discussing resistance as a community right. Resistance to oppression was, to be sure, both a personal and community right. Hamilton reminded his countrymen in *A Full Vindication* that "self-preservation is the first principle of our nature," and other writers, following Blackstone and Grotius, asserted the unalienability of the great law of self-defense. A man could not bargain away for any equivalent his ultimate right to use force to meet unlawful force, whether it be the pistol of a highwayman or the decree of a wicked judge. For the most part, however, American thinkers devoted their attention to the causes and techniques of large-scale, public resistance to arbitrary power and ignored the unalienable right of the individual to defend his life, liberty, and property against illegal force. A South Carolinian spoke of "those *latent,* though *inherent* rights of SOCIETY, which *no climate, no time, no constitution, no contract,* can ever destroy or diminish," and Jefferson wrote in his *Summary View* of "those sacred and sovereign rights of punishment, reserved in the hands of the people for cases of extreme necessity, and judged by the constitution unsafe to be delegated to any other judicature."

American writers, constitutionalists all, placed special

emphasis on the broken contract as justification for community resistance. The will of God, the Old and New Testaments, nature, history, and the British Constitution all sanctioned popular resistance to oppressive authority, but the one clear occasion for exercising this right was the breaking of the original contract, "the overleaping the bounds of the fundamental law." The General Court of Massachusetts tied together the contract and resistance in its proclamation of January 23, 1776:

As the happiness of the people is the sole end of government, so the consent of the people is the only foundation of it, in reason, morality, and the natural fitness of things. And therefore every act of government, every exercise of sovereignty, against, or without, the consent of the people, is injustice, usurpation, and tyranny. . . .

When kings, ministers, governors, or legislators, therefore, instead of exercising the powers entrusted with them, according to the principles, forms and proportions stated by the constitution, and established by the original compact, prostitute those powers to the purposes of oppression—to subvert, instead of supporting a free constitution;—to destroy, instead of preserving the lives, liberties and properties of the people; —they are no longer to be deemed magistrates vested with a sacred character, but become public enemies, and ought to be resisted.

The grand jury for 1776 in Georgetown, South Carolina, expressed a similar notion:

When a People . . . find that, by the baseness and corruption of their rulers, those laws which were intended as the guardians of their sacred and unalienable rights, are impiously perverted into instruments of oppression; and, in violation of every social compact, and the ties of common justice, every means is adopted by those whom they instituted to govern and protect them, to enslave and destroy them: human nature and the laws of God justify their employing those means for redress which self-preservation dictates.

And Chief Justice Drayton of the same colony identified the contract and the parties to it by stating:

The house of Brunswick was yet scarcely settled in the British throne, to which it had been called by a free people, when, in the year 1719, our ancestors in this country, finding that the government of the lords proprietors operated to their ruin, exercised the rights transmitted to them by their forefathers of England; and casting off the proprietary authority, called upon the house of Brunswick to rule over them—a house elevated to royal dominion, for no other purpose than to preserve to a people their unalienable rights. The king accepted the invitation, and thereby indisputably admitted the legality of that revolution. And in so doing, by his own act, he vested in those our forefathers, and us their posterity, a clear right to effect *another* revolution, if ever the government of the house of Brunswick should operate to the ruin of the people.

From this identification of South Carolina's contract with the Kings of England, Drayton moved ahead to document fully—by comparing the actions of James II and George III—those breaches which permitted the colonists to renounce their allegiance. In doing this he followed the lead of several more important thinkers, all of whom were anxious to prove that the King had "unkinged" himself by breaking the contract. Although Drayton and the others agreed that God and nature had granted the right of resistance to every man and community for self-defense against arbitrary force of any kind, they preferred to treat this right as the whole people's final remedy against one specific show of force:

the grossly unconstitutional actions of covenanted rulers.

Resistance to illegal authority, not rebellion or revolution, was the only right and purpose of the American colonists. The emphasis their spokesmen placed on the broken contract permitted them to deny absolutely that they were rebellious in nature or revolutionary in intent. It was all as simple as this: They had contracted away— not irrevocably—their original power to govern themselves. They were meeting the harsh fact of a major breach of the contract by resuming this power and granting it to others on new terms. The rulers who had exercised unlawful authority were the real rebels. The people were merely exercising, Rev. Gad Hitchcock pointed out, "the right of saving themselves from ruin." Scores of letters and pamphlets developed a theme especially appealing to American minds, which was well stated in a letter of 1774 from Pacificus to Tranquillus in the *Pennsylvania Gazette:*

I readily agree with you, Sir, that the crime of rebellion is of the deepest dye, and in every civil war, doubtless one side or the other are rebels; but if that be the only government pleasing to God or useful to man, which maintains the peace, safety and happiness of the people, and if no good reason can be assigned to induce any rational creature to become a member of that community which denies these blessings to its members, then I would ask, who are the rebels in any contest of the kind, the governors who abuse the trust reposed in them, and exercise the delegated power of the people to their hurt; or the governed, who attempt to protect themselves against the abuse of that power?

If subjection is only due to a legal exertion of power, and if power ought only to be employed for the good of the community, then he alone is chargeable with rebellion, who uses the power he possesses to the hurt of the people, and not the people, who oppose every illegal exertion of that power.

"Our enemies falsely charged us," The Monitor said in 1775 in John Holt's *New-York Journal,*

with endeavouring to subvert the Constitution; but upon the fairest examination, it must be evident, that we are its truest supporters; while they are its most flagitious destroyers. . . .

If the Constitution is to be the touchstone of Treason and Rebellion, and the violators of it are the Traitors and Rebels, then will those appellations belong more properly to the Ministry and their instruments, who are labouring to overturn it, than to us, who are making every possible exertion in support of its purest principles?

Virginians made excellent practical use of this distinction. When their last royal Governor, Lord Dunmore, proclaimed them to be in rebellion, they retorted immediately in public print that he was the rebel and they the saviors of the constitution. "By the frame of our constitution, the duties of protection and allegiance are reciprocal." Since the Governor had withdrawn his protection, Virginians could withdraw their allegiance.

Resistance to unlawful authority, to breaches of the original contract, was more than just a right and "a Virtue." The Provincial Congress reminded the inhabitants of Massachusetts in 1775 that it was "the Christian and social duty of each Individual," and Rev. John Allen argued:

It is no rebellion to oppose any King, ministry, or governor, that destroys by any violence or authority whatever, the rights of the people. Shall a man be deem'd a rebel that supports his own rights? It is the first law of nature, and he must be a rebel to GOD, to the laws of nature, and his own conscience, who will not do it.

In short, "the man who refuses to assert his right to liberty, property, and life, is guilty of the worst kind of rebellion; he commits high treason against *God*." Hardly less important to this history-conscious people, he is a betrayer of generations yet unborn:

Honor, justice, and *humanity* call upon us to hold, and to transmit to our posterity, that liberty which we received from our ancestors. It is not our duty to leave wealth to our children; but it is our duty to leave liberty to them. No infamy, iniquity, or cruelty, can exceed our own, if we, born and educated in a country of freedom, entitled to its blessings, and knowing their value, pusillanimously deserting the post assigned us by Divine Providence, surrender succeeding generations to a condition of wretchedness, from which no human efforts, in all probability, will be sufficient to extricate them.

American thinkers revealed their conservative orientation in other refinements or qualifications of the right of resistance. First, they rejected flatly the stock Tory argument that to admit the right of resistance was simply to invite political and social instability. "Quite the contrary," replied an unknown author in the *Salem Gazette,* who wrote "For the Perusal of Lord NORTH":

People are not so easily got out of their old forms as some are apt to suggest; they are hardly to be prevailed with to amend the acknowledged faults in the frame they have been accustomed to. . . .
Such revolutions happen not upon every little mismanagement in public affairs. Great mistakes in the ruling party, and many wrong laws, and slips of human frailty, will be borne by the people; but if a long train of abuses and artifices, all

tending the same way, make the design visible to the people, and they see whither they are going, it is not to be wondered that they should then rouse themselves, for specious names and forms are worse than the state of nature or pure anarchy.

Jefferson emphasized this point in the preamble to the Declaration of Independence. He, too, made use of the Lockean phrase, "a long train of abuses," to describe the circumstances necessary to overcome mankind's disposition "to suffer, while evils are sufferable, than to right themselves by abolishing the forms to which they are accustomed." Far from being turbulent, restless, and seditious, the people, even though aware of their right to resist, were not half so likely to violate the terms of the contract as were their governors and magistrates. As Samuel Cooke put it:

The history of past ages and of our nation shows that the greatest dangers have arisen from lawless power. The body of a people are disposed to lead quiet and peaceable lives, and it is their highest interest to support the government under which their quietness is ensured. They retain a reverence for their superiors, and seldom foresee or suspect danger till they feel their burdens.

Therefore, added the aptly named Pacificus in the *Pennsylvania Gazette,* there must be

a strong presumption against the supreme magistrate and his creatures, in every contest of this nature; for it is scarcely credible that the community would revolt from that power which they knew to be exerted for their good; or that they would withdraw their allegiance from the governor, who exercised the authority with which they had invested him, purely for their service.

Second, the people had a solemn duty to be peaceful and law-abiding. Rev. Charles Turner spoke for a large majority when he warned:

The people ought to have the end of government, the publick good, at heart, as well as the magistrate; and therefore, to yield all loyal subjection to well regulated government, in opposition to every thing of a factious nature and complexion.

Force was the people's final defense, but force, wrote "John Locke" to the people of Boston in 1765,

is to be opposed only to unjust and unlawful force; whoever makes any opposition in any other case, draws on himself a just condemnation both from GOD and man.

Third, the nature and extent of resistance was to be determined by the nature and extent of oppression. Petty tyranny called for passive resistance; premeditated despotism called for active resistance. Resistance in the extreme sense of outright revolution—the "appeal to God by the sword," as the Colony of New Hampshire labeled it—was never to be undertaken except by an overwhelming majority of a thoroughly abused people. There was no place in Revolutionary thought for the *coup d'état* of a militant minority dedicated to the building of a new order. Samuel West expressed this thought in his election sermon of 1776:

If it be asked, who are the proper judges to determine, when rulers are guilty of tyranny and oppression? I answer, the publick; not a few disaffected individuals, but the collective body of the state must decide this question.

Finally, all American writers agreed with Jefferson's assumption that any exercise of "the Right of the People to alter or to abolish" government would be followed almost immediately by an exercise of their associated right "to institute new Government." For all their flirtation with the state of nature, for all their loyalty to the mechanistic explanation of government, Americans could think of man only as a member of a political community. Men did not revolt against government to eliminate it entirely and return to a state of nature, but to organize a new one, "laying its foundation on such principles and organizing its powers in such form, as to them shall seem most likely to effect their Safety and Happiness." God granted men the right of resistance to help them preserve orderly constitutional government, not to induce them to fly from the tyranny of arbitrary power to the tyranny of no power at all.

The right of resistance to arbitrary power was, in sum, the last resort of a people unable to protect their lives, liberties, and properties by normal constitutional methods. It was a right to be exercised only by an overwhelming majority of the community against rulers who had so completely ignored the terms of the original contract as to make further allegiance a crime against God and reason. Indeed, resistance was not so much the right as the solemn, unpleasant duty of a betrayed people. Thus did the conservative, law-abiding, constitutional Americans reason about the use of force in defense of liberty. Never have a people engaged in revolution been so anxious to convince themselves and the world that they were not really revolutionaries at all. Chief Justice Drayton of South Carolina expressed the legalism and conservatism of American thinking about the act of resistance when he announced to his grand jury, April 23, 1776, that George III had "unkinged" himself:

And thus, as I have on the foot of the best authorities made it evident, that George the third, king of Great Britain, has endeavored to subvert the constitution of this country, by breaking the original contract between king and people; by the advice of wicked persons, has violated the fundamental laws, and has withdrawn himself, by withdrawing the constitutional benefits of the kingly office, and his protection out of this country: From such a result of injuries, from such a conjuncture of circumstances—the law of the land authorises me to declare, and it is my duty boldly to declare the law, that George the third, king of Great Britain, has abdicated the government, and that the throne is thereby vacant; that is, HE HAS NO AUTHORITY OVER US, and WE OWE NO OBEDIENCE TO HIM.

Three

THE PATTERN OF GOVERNMENT

The political philosophy of anarchy is concerned almost exclusively with the rights of the individual, the political philosophy of autocracy with the purposes of the state. The quest of the one is absolute liberty; the passion of the other is absolute order. The political philosophy of the American Revolution was a notable attempt to strike a balance between these equally dangerous and repulsive extremes. It was a philosophy of ordered liberty, of the free yet dependent person in the sheltering yet compulsive community. The men who expounded this system of ideas were therefore as concerned with the pattern of government as with the rights of man. Convinced that the concept of man without government was valid only as a useful hypothesis or a fact of prehistory, they gave nearly as much attention to political organization as to political liberty. We have heard what they had to say about man—about his nature, his rights, and the higher law that governs and protects him. Now we are to hear them speak about government—about its origin, purpose, nature, structure, and moral basis. Yet even as we divide Revolutionary political thought into the prime categories of man and government, we must again recall that these halves made up an indivisible whole. In theory as in fact, man and government could not exist apart from one another.

American speculation about political organization went through three stages in the decade before independence. In the first few years most writers were quite unimaginative, apparently content to parrot the teachings of the great Whigs about the origin and purpose of government and the beauties of the English Constitution. Around 1770, in a few instances even earlier, their writings began to show increased independence of judgment. And finally, in 1775 and 1776, thinking Americans embarked upon a campaign of constructive thought that was to lead through the first state constitutions to the Convention of 1787 and from there to the triumph of constitutional republicanism in the Federalist and Jeffersonian periods. Rarely have men been privileged to think such influential thoughts about the purpose and form of government. As the most constructive political thinker of the era, John Adams, observed to a colleague in greatness, George Wythe:

You and I, my dear friend, have been sent into life at a time when the greatest lawgivers of antiquity would have wished to live. How few of the human race have ever enjoyed an opportunity of making an election of government, more than of air, soil, or climate, for themselves or their children! When, before the present epocha, had three millions of people full power and a fair opportunity to form and establish the wisest and happiest government that human wisdom can contrive?

And rarely has such a measure of practical success crowned the speculative efforts of a school of political thought.

TEN

The Origin, Purpose,
and Nature of Government

REVOLUTIONARY THINKERS followed a well-worn path to a standard explanation of the origin of government. The concept of the contract or compact is nearly as old as political theory itself, and we have already noted the universality of its appeal to early Americans. The men of the Revolution honored all their past in clinging to the belief that men institute government as an act of will. Their lack of originality in handling this crucial problem of political theory was a tribute to the vigor and utility of a great tradition rather than a sign of mental indolence or incuriosity.

The opening pages of *Common Sense* present one of the most precise renditions of the mechanistic theory in Revolutionary literature. Although many American thinkers disagreed strongly with Paine's unrelenting belief that the "rise of government" results solely from "the inability of moral virtue to govern the world," almost all of them subscribed to some such explanation as this:

In order to gain a clear and just idea of the design and end of government, let us suppose a small number of persons settled in some sequestered part of the earth, unconnected with the rest; they will then represent the first peopling of any country, or of the world. In this state of natural liberty, society will be their first thought. A thousand motives will excite them thereto; the strength of one man is so unequal to his wants, and his mind so unfitted for perpetual solitude, that he is soon obliged to seek assistance and relief of another, who in his turn requires the same. . . .

Thus necessity, like a gravitating power, would soon form our newly arrived emigrants into society, the reciprocal blessings of which would supersede and render the obligations of law and government unnecessary while they remained perfectly just to each other; but as nothing but heaven is impregnable to vice, it will unavoidably happen that in proportion as they surmount the first difficulties of emigration, which bound them together in a common cause, they will begin to relax in their duty and attachment to each other; and this remissness will point out the necessity of establishing some form of government to supply the defect of moral virtue.

Some convenient tree will afford them a statehouse, under the branches of which the whole colony may assemble to deliberate on public matters. It is more than probable that their first laws will have the title only of REGULATIONS and be enforced by no other penalty than public disesteem. In this first parliament every man by natural right will have a seat.

But as the colony increases, the public concerns will increase likewise, and the distance at which the members may be separated will render it too inconvenient for all of them to meet on every occasion as at first, when their number was small, their habitations near, and the public concerns few and trifling. This will point out the convenience of their consenting to leave the legislative part to be managed by a select number chosen from the whole body, who are supposed to have the same concerns at stake which those have who appointed them, and who will act in the same manner as the whole body would act were they present.

Paine's account is especially important for its careful distinction between society and government. While some thinkers confounded these two aspects of the total community, the best of them agreed with Paine that these were different levels of organization with "different origins." Society was the involuntary, unconscious, natural result of the presence of a group of men "in the midst of a wilderness." Man's need for companionship as well as for "assistance and relief" made society rather than isolation his natural condition. The true state of nature was not an area full of hermits or self-sustaining families, but a community in which men lived and worked together without government, in Locke's famous words, "without a common superior on earth . . . to judge between them." Government, too, was a natural institution, but with this difference: The vital questions—Who shall govern? For what purposes? Through what methods?—were to be answered by men capable of exercising free choice. If nature forced men to submit to government, it left them free to decide upon its form and personnel, and they might therefore properly insist, as did Rev. John Tucker, that it was "the *ordinance of men—an human institution.*"

This, then, was the contract in Revolutionary thought: an agreement of free and equal men, not to enter into society, but to institute government on terms mutually satisfactory to them and their prospective rulers. Having agreed among themselves to form a government—a step they had to take whether they liked it or not—they then agreed upon its structure, functions, powers, and limitations. Finally, they bargained with one or more wise men to rule them, at the same time making clear that all future rulers would become parties to this contract upon entering office. The first contract was a promise among free men to respect and sustain one another; the second was a promise of free men to give allegiance and of wise men to extend protection. Actually, the two contracts— of man with man and of men with their governors— were one. When Revolutionary thinkers talked of "the social compact," they meant an agreement to form government, not society.

Americans used the words "compact," "contract," or "covenant" to refer to several situations of actual bargaining or constitution-making:

The original charters and their many renewals. (This assumption made it necessary to argue that the first colonists had exercised the natural right of migration, had settled the wilderness "at their own Expence, & not the Nations," and had then contracted voluntarily with the sovereign left behind.)

The agreement with William and Mary, in which the colonists joined, upon their accession following the Glorious Revolution.

The continuous agreement through which, John Adams wrote, "America has all along consented, still consents, and ever will consent, that parliament, being the most powerful legislature in the dominions, should regulate the trade of the dominions."

A possible new agreement with the King, which would adjust all outstanding differences and contain a renewed promise of popular allegiance and royal protection.

The many associations, leagues, covenants, and other pledges of faith into which various groups of colonists entered in this decade of crisis.

The new state constitutions and, in time, the Articles of Confederation and Constitution of 1787.

The idea of the contract was especially serviceable in the first of these instances. It brought new dignity and meaning to the charters themselves; it provided philosophical and historical support for the dominion theory implicit in the Declaration of Independence. An argument such as this one in the *Boston Gazette* in 1766 was extremely convincing to American minds:

When the first settlers of this country had transplanted themselves here, they were to be considered, either as in a state of nature, or else as subjects of that kingdom from whence they had migrated: If they were in the state of nature, they were then entitled to all the rights of nature. . . . They had a right to erect a government upon what form they thought best; or to connect themselves, for the sake of their own advantage and security, either with the natives or any other people upon the globe, who were willing to be connected with them: It is a fact, that they chose to erect a government of their own, much under the same form, as that was, which they had formerly been under in Europe; and chose the King of England for *their* King. . . . The people here still remain under the most sacred tie, the subjects of the *King* of Great Britain; but utterly unaccountable to, & uncontroulable by the *people* of Great Britain, or any body of them whatever; their compact being with the King only, to him alone they submitted, to be govern'd by him, agreeable to the terms of that compact, contained in their charter.

Designation of the charter as an original contract permitted orators like John Allen to ask indignantly:

I would be glad to know, my Lord, what right the King of England has to America? it cannot be an hereditary right, that lies in Hanover, it cannot be a parliamentary right, that lies in Britain, not a victorious right. . . . Then he can have no more right to America, than what the people have by compact, invested him with, which is only a power to protect them, and defend their rights civil and religious; and to sign, seal, and confirm, as their steward, such laws as the people of America shall consent to.

The men of the Revolution were convinced that they, like their ancestors, were happily privileged to form new compacts. The Continental Congress appealed to the inhabitants of Quebec in 1774 "to unite with us in one social compact, formed on the generous principles of equal liberty, and cemented by such an exchange of beneficial and endearing offices as to render it perpetual." The Massachusetts Constitution of 1780 stated:

The body politic is formed by a voluntary association of individuals. It is a social compact, by which the whole people covenant with each citizen, and each citizen with the whole people, that all shall be governed by certain laws for the common good.

And the men of Massachusetts, in adopting the Constitution of the United States in 1788, acknowledged

with grateful hearts the goodness of the Supreme Ruler of the Universe, in affording the people of the United States, in the course of his providence, an opportunity, deliberately and peaceably, without fraud or surprise, of entering into an explicit and solemn compact with each other, by assenting to and ratifying a new constitution.

These and dozens of other practical applications of the doctrine of contract make clear that Americans were determined to be the one people in a hundred of whom James Otis had written:

The form of government is by *nature* and by *right* so far left to the individuals of each society, that they may alter it from a simple democracy or government of all over all, to any other form they please. Such alteration may and ought to be made by express compact: But how seldom this right has been asserted, history will abundantly show. For once that it has been fairly settled by compact; *fraud force or accident* have determined it an hundred times.

The contract was as effective a tool in the construction of the new order of independence as it had been in the destruction of the old order of empire.

But the contract was something more than a clever contrivance with which propagandists could rewrite the past and dignify the present. It was the substance and symbol of the American solution to the problem of obligation, the most perplexing problem in the political theory of freedom, since it poses such questions as: Why do men submit to the compulsions of government? By what authority does government bind men with positive laws? How can men call themselves free if they are subject to a concentration of political power that can restrict their liberty, deprive them of their property, even take away their lives?

To these and other questions of political obligation Revolutionary thinkers advanced a one-word answer as satisfying to them as it was distasteful to their adversaries: *consent.* Men obeyed government because they had consented to obey it. Through the original contract they had exchanged allegiance and obedience for protection and peace. They had agreed to certain well-defined

restrictions on their natural freedom as part of a scheme
for securing the rest of that freedom against the whims
and jealousies of the men with whom they lived. At the
same time, they had agreed to representative institutions,
notably the legislative assembly and jury of peers, through
which they could continue to consent to necessary restrictions on liberty and property. Government, the community organized for political purposes, could restrict
men's liberty, deprive them of their property, even take
away their lives, because it did all this with their original
and continuing consent. The power of government to do
these things was not intrinsic but derived, and derived
from the free consent of the very people it governed. In
short, the American answer to this troublesome question
was simply that the only valid obligation to obey government is self-obligation. *"Resolved,"* voted the freeholders and other inhabitants of Mendon, Massachusetts,
in 1773, "That all just and lawful Government must
necessarily originate in the free Consent of the People."
The obsession of Americans with the principle of consent
is evident in two representative discussions of the relation
of political authority to private property in the press of
Massachusetts.

From the *Boston Gazette,* November 18, 1765:

No government can have a RIGHT to obedience from a
people, who have not *freely consented* to it; which they can
never be supposed to do, till either they are put in a full state
of *liberty* to choose their government and governors, or at
least till they have such standing laws to which they have by
themselves or their *representatives given their consent,* and
also, till they are allowed their due *property,* which is so to be
proprietors of what they have, that no body can take away
any *part* of it without their *consent,* without which men un-

der any government are not in the *state of freedom,* but are *direct slaves,* under the force of war. The nature of *property* is, that without a man's own consent it cannot be taken from him.

From the *Salem Gazette,* August 19, 1774:

The supreme power cannot take from any man any part of his property without his own consent; for the preservation of property being the end of government, and that for which men enter into society; it necessarily requires that the people should have property, without which they must be supposed to lose that by entering into society, which was the end for which they entered into it; too gross an absurdity for any man to own. . . .

It is true, government cannot be supported without great charge, and 'tis fit that every one who enjoys protection should pay out of his estate his proportion for the support of it; but still it must be done with his own consent, or by his representative chosen by him, for if any one shall lay and levy taxes by his own authority, and without such consent of the people, he thereby invades the fundamental law of property, and subverts the end of government, for what property have I in that which another may by right take when he pleases to himself?

To these revealing comments should be added the definition of political liberty in the *Essex Result:*

Let it be thus defined; political liberty is the right every man in the state has, to do whatever is not prohibited by laws, TO WHICH HE HAS GIVEN HIS CONSENT. This definition is in unison with the feelings of a free people.

The notion of consent doubtless had a good deal more appeal to "the feelings of a free people" than to the reasoning powers of their philosophers; yet if sophisticated exponents of the American consensus were troubled by the dangers and ambiguities of this notion, they failed to reveal it in their pamphlets, sermons, and letters. The great framework of Anglo-American constitutionalism— charters, constitutions, bills of rights, elections, assemblies, juries, representation, common law, limited prerogative, majority rule—seemed to them to be rationalized only by the principle of popular consent. This principle, in turn, found rationalization in the contract, the symbol of political obligation derived from free consent. In this sense, the contract was the logical justification rather than historical explanation of the existence and authority of the political community. It answered the great question— What authority should government exercise?—by stating: the authority that free and reasonable men consent to its exercising. If consent was the key to limited and popular government, the compact was the key to consent. Only thus, a citizen of Connecticut wrote in 1770, could men secure "mutual harmony, unanimity and concord . . . the great cement and connecting bands of human society."

A corollary of the contractual origin of government was the doctrine of popular sovereignty, a very simple solution to a very complex problem. American thinkers, unlike many of their children and grandchildren, were generally ready to concur in Blackstone's dictum that in all governments "there is and must be . . . a supreme, irresistible, uncontrolled authority, in which the *jura summi imperii,* or the rights of sovereignty, reside," but they were quick to add that in all free governments this authority resided in the people. In a proclamation dated January 23, 1776, the General Court of Massachusetts announced:

It is a maxim that in every government, there must exist, somewhere, a supreme, sovereign, absolute, and uncontrolable power; but this power resides always in the body of the people; and it never was, or can be delegated to one man, or a few; the great Creator having never given to men a right to vest others with authority over them unlimited either in duration or degree.

Blackstone, of course, had been speaking of *legal* sovereignty, of "a supreme, irresistible, uncontrolled authority" residing in government itself. The Americans, on the other hand, were speaking of *political sovereignty*, of the ultimate source from which all legitimate power must be derived. Some of them were quite uninterested in legal sovereignty; others, like James Wilson, were prepared to deny its existence. All of them agreed that even the sovereign people were to be guided and restricted by the laws of nature in exercising their original authority. Political sovereignty was "supreme, irresistible, uncontrolled" only within the sphere assigned to it in the great plan of nature.

In short, the Americans, to the extent that they thought about the problem at all, rejected the concept of supreme legal sovereignty in favor of limited political sovereignty. To the observation that "limited sovereignty" was a contradiction in terms, they would doubtless have replied that they proposed to define their terms to suit themselves. By insisting so vigorously on the necessity and viability of limited government, they actually converted "sovereignty" into a virtually meaningless term. Whatever their conclusions about the scope of political power, all shared the belief expressed by General Washington in a letter of August 19, 1775, to General Gage:

I cannot conceive [of authority] more honourable, than that which flows from the uncorrupted choice of a brave and free people—the purest source and original fountain of all power.

In the process of denying parliamentary and asserting provincial or independent authority, American thinkers had a good deal to say about the purpose of government. Most were in accord with Hamilton, Paine, and Otis that the purpose of society was to extend to each man in it, in return for his talents and exertions, the benefits of the strength, skills, and benevolence of the other men with whom he was associated. The purpose of government, however, evoked a more varied range of comment. Here, in the words of some of the leading thinkers, were the reasons why men chose to submit to government:

Samuel Adams, rejecting the doctrine of taxation without representation:

It destroys the very end for which alone man can be supposed to submit to civil government, which is not for the sake of exalting one man, or a few men above their equals, that they may be maintained in splendour and greatness; but that each individual, under the joint protection of the whole community, may be the Lord of his own possession, and sit securely under his own vine.

Hampden, in "The Alarm" (1773):

The chief End of all free Government, is the Protection of Property. . . . Property is here used in the Large Sense in which Mr. Locke used it, as comprehending Life, Liberty, and Estate.

A gentleman writing "From the County of Hampshire" to the *Massachusetts Spy* in 1775:

Personal liberty, personal security, and private property are the three only motives, the grand objects for which individuals make a partial surrender of that plenitude of power which they possess in a state of nature, and submit to the necessary restrictions, and subordinations of government.

Spartanus, on "The Interest of America," in the *New-Hampshire Gazette,* June 15, 1776:

Let us now consider what men *relinquish,* and what they *obtain,* by passing out of a state of nature, and entering into society, or a state of civil government. 1st.—They give up their right to judge between themselves and those that offend or injure them, and leave this to the civil magistrate; consequently they give up the right to vindicate or revenge themselves, any other way than by the magistrate or proper officers. 2d.—They give up part of their estates, for the support of government. 3d.—They are under obligation to expose their lives for the safety of the state when necessary, and when called upon to do it. If money will not answer, each man must bear his proper part in the defence of the whole. The proper support of government, supposes that we are ready, with our lives and fortunes, to engage in it's defense. Shall it now be asked, what we obtain by entering into civil government? I answer we gain *protection,* the protection of our lives and properties; that we may without violence enjoy our *own.*

Rev. Samuel Cooke:

In a civil state, that form is most eligible which is best adapted to promote the ends of government—the benefit of the community.

John Adams:

Government is a frame, a scheme, a system, a combination of powers for a certain end, namely,—the good of the whole community. The public good, the *Salus populi,* is the professed end of all government.

The Continental Congress:

A reverence for our great Creator, principles of humanity, and the dictates of common sense, must convince all those who reflect upon the subject, that government was instituted to promote the welfare of mankind, and ought to be administered for the attainment of that end.

James Wilson:

All lawful government is founded on the consent of those who are subject to it: such consent was given with a view to ensure and encrease the happiness of the governed. . . . The consequence is, that the happiness of the society is the *first* law of every government.

James Iredell:

The object of all government is, or ought to be, *the happiness of the people governed.*

And finally, the people of Mendon, Massachusetts, in 1773:

Resolved, That the Good, Safety and Happiness of the People, is the great End of civil Government; and must be considered as the only rational Object, in all original Compacts, and political Institutions.

One major point of agreement and one of disagreement appears in this variety of opinions about the purpose of government. Americans agreed almost unanimously that government existed only for the benefit of the men who had submitted to it. Even when they used such collective phrases as "the welfare of mankind," "the public good," and "the benefit of the community," they were thinking in terms of the welfare, good, or benefit of each individual. Government had no purpose of its own. The only purpose that counted was that of the men who had instituted it: to seek protection for their "personal liberty, personal security, and private property."

The major point of disagreement, of which few thinkers were fully conscious, was between those who continued to emphasize the protection of life, liberty, and property and those who now began to look upon government as an agency designed "to ensure and encrease the happiness of the governed." Wilson, Iredell, and Jefferson were among those who moved beyond Locke to proclaim, however vaguely, a more positive purpose for the political community. It is doubtful that any one of these men, even the clear-headed Wilson, realized how revolutionary a step it was to salute the pursuit of happiness as a natural right to be protected and even encouraged by government. Nevertheless, it is worth observing that a few imaginative Americans, most of whom seem to have picked up the notion from Burlamaqui, added a new right to man's natural heritage and thus a new dimension to government. And if they spoke occasionally of the happiness of the community as a chief end of government, they meant the happiness of all the persons who had consented to it. Revolutionary thinkers were completely oriented to individualism in their discussions of the purpose of the political community.

Those two supposedly like-minded rabble-rousers, Tom Paine and Sam Adams, were actually some distance apart on several important points. Certainly they had different opinions about the nature of government. Paine based much of his philosophy on the fundamental assumption that "government, even in its best state, is but a necessary evil"; Adams considered it "an ordinance of Heaven, design'd by the all-benevolent Creator, for the general happiness of his rational creature, man." Which one expressed more accurately the prevailing sentiment of the time? Was government a *good* institution for which men could thank wise Providence, or an *evil* one for which they could blame their own moral insufficiencies?

The answer is that Adams spoke for an overwhelming majority of American opinion, Paine for few men other than himself. A scattering of preachers like Judah Champion voiced much the same opinion as the opening pages of *Common Sense,* but most thinkers, lay and clerical, rejected the notion that there was something intrinsically evil about government. The assumption that government was, as Rev. Jonas Clarke wrote, "this richest of temporal blessings to mankind" generally proceeded from these other assumptions about its inherent nature: that it was natural, necessary, and derived.

The concept of government as a natural institution was the obvious corollary to the concept of man as a social and political animal. "Certain it is," R. H. Lee wrote, "that there is nothing more becoming to human nature than well-ordered government." "Civil government is founded in the very nature of man, as a social being, and in the nature and constitution of things," Rev. John Tucker stated. "It is manifestly for the good of society." Civil government, John Adams echoed, is "founded in nature and reason." And James Otis, always something of a maverick, went so far as to say, "*Government* is . . . most evidently founded *on the necessities of our nature.* It is by no means an *arbitrary* thing, depending merely on *compact* or *human will* for its existence." Even those writers who emphasized the importance of "compact or human will" in the formulation of government agreed that men were impelled "to covenant each with the other" by an irresistible, higher force. Civil government, Stephen Johnson announced, was "the dictate of reason, of nature, and the will of God." Government was artificial only in the sense that men had some control over its structure and complete control over its personnel.

If government was good because it was natural, it was natural because it was necessary. James Otis expressed this sentiment in his *Rights of the British Colonies:*

The *end* of government being the *good* of mankind, points out its great duties: It is above all things to provide for the security, the quiet, and happy enjoyment of life, liberty, and property. There is no one act which a government can have a *right* to make, that does not tend to the advancement of the security, tranquility and prosperity of the people. If life, liberty and property could be enjoyed in as great perfection in *solitude,* as in *society,* there would be no need of government. But the experience of ages has proved that such is the nature of man, a weak, imperfect being; that the valuable ends of life cannot be obtained without the union and assistance of many. Hence 'tis clear that men cannot live apart or independent of each other: In solitude men would perish; and yet they cannot live together without contests. These contests require some arbitrator to determine them. The necessity of a common, indifferent and impartial judge, makes all men seek one.

Paine found government a necessary evil since "produced by our wickedness." Otis found it a necessary good since produced by our wants. The men of Massachusetts were inclined to agree with Otis. Said the General Court in 1776:

The frailty of human nature, the wants of individuals, and the numerous dangers which surround them, through the course of life, have, in all ages, and in every country, impelled them to form societies and establish governments.

Good government was something more than a punitive agency. Even if men should become angels, some political organization would be necessary to adjust, of course without compulsion, the complexity of human (or angelic) relations and to do for the people what they could not do as individuals or families. If Revolutionary spokesmen had no vision of the welfare or insurance state, neither did they subscribe to the concept of government as "anarchy plus a street constable."

The men of the Revolution would have been quite unconvinced by the argument that it is a dangerous thing to consider government an inherently good, even divine institution. Government, they would have answered, can be safely acknowledged a temporal blessing because, in terms of the power it wields, there is nothing inherent about it. Government is not an end in itself but the means to an end. Its authority is the free and revocable grant of the men who have promised conditionally to submit to it. Its organs, however ancient and august, are instruments that free men have built and free men can alter or even abolish. Government can be arbitrary, corrupt, oppressive, wicked—but not if men are conscious of its origin, purpose, proper limits, and source of authority. Indeed, tyranny is not government but an abuse of government. True government is a good, natural, necessary institution ordained by providence to serve man's higher earthly purposes. An anonymous writer in the *Pennsylvania Evening Post*, May 16, 1776, expressed the firm belief of most Revolutionary thinkers:

Q. What is government?

A. Certain powers vested by society in public persons for the security, peace, and happiness of its members.

Q. What ought a society to do to secure a good government?

A. Any thing. The happiness of man, as an inhabitant of this world, depends intirely upon it.

In conclusion to this chapter, we might note two facts about Revolutionary discussions of society and government: first, that many writers who should have been more careful used these words interchangeably, thereby befogging the vital and acknowledged distinction between the two levels or stages of the community; second, that the colonists had no theory of the state in the modern sense. While they occasionally used this word to denote society or government or the total community, they did not conceive of the state as a third entity that embraced, yet stood apart from, the two natural types of human association. And this, of course, permitted them to argue that sovereignty remained fixed and absolutely unalienable in the people—a useful point of view for revolutionists to adopt.

ELEVEN

The Imperatives
of Good Government: I

"THE BLESSINGS OF SOCIETY," John Adams wrote to George Wythe, "depend entirely on the constitutions of government." Government might be good and necessary, but like all other gifts of God and nature it was subject to abuse. The pages of history bore grim witness to the fact that government could be so far abused as to defeat rather than gratify the purpose of its institution. Phillips Payson warned his listeners:

Much depends upon the mode and administration of civil government to complete the blessings of liberty; for although the best possible plan of government never can give an ignorant and vicious people the true enjoyment of liberty, yet a state may be enslaved though its inhabitants in general may be knowing, virtuous, and heroic.

Government, if not corrupt, was corruptible. The business of "the divine science of politics" was to discover the form least likely to be corrupted and most likely to fulfill the accepted ends of the free political community. "We ought to consider," John Adams meditated,

what is the end of government, before we determine which is the best form. Upon this point all speculative politicians will agree, that the happiness of society is the end of government, as all divines and moral philosophers will agree that the happiness of the individual is the end of man. From this principle it will follow, that the form of government which communicates ease, comfort, security, or, in one word, happiness, to the greatest number of persons, and in the greatest degree, is the best.

Or as "Spartanus" stated the issue in the *New-Hampshire Gazette*:

The important day is come, or near at hand, that America is to assume a form of government for herself. We should be very desirous to know what form is best.—And that surely is best which is most natural, easy, cheap, and which best secures the rights of the people. We should always keep in mind that great truth, viz. That the good of the people is the ultimate end of civil Government.

To hit upon and help initiate this ideal form of government was the consuming passion of men like Adams in the years immediately before and after independence. After generations of slavish, uncritical praise of the English system of government, they were now, as if for the first time, forced to consider candidly the problem of political organization. For the most part, they seemed delighted with the opportunity thrust upon them. Said John Witherspoon:

All the governments we have read of in former ages were settled by caprice or accident, by the influence of prevailing parties or particular persons, or prescribed by a conqueror.

Important improvements indeed have been forced upon some constitutions by the spirit of daring men, supported by successful insurrections. But to see government in large and populous countries settled from its foundation by deliberate counsel, and directed immediately to the public good of the present and future generations . . . is certainly altogether new.

If Americans were not quite the free agents they fancied themselves, still they had more right than most men to boast with Spartanus:

We have opportunity to form with some deliberation, with free choice, with good advantages for knowledge; we have opportunity to observe what has been right, and what wrong in other states, and to profit by them.

Before we examine the constitutional thought of the Revolutionary period, we should call attention to the emotional context in which the Americans spun out their new plans of government. Two passages are representative of the spirit of the times.

Our old friend Spartanus:

The affair now in view is the most important that ever was before America. In my opinion it is the most important that has been transacted in any nation for some centuries past. If our civil Government is well constructed, and well managed, America bids fair to be the most glorious state that has ever been on earth. We should now at the beginning lay the foundation right.

Salus Populi in the *New-York Packet*, March 28, 1776:

I cannot help cherishing a secret hope that God has destined America to form the last and best plan that can possibly exist, and that he will gradually carry those who have long been under the galling yoke of tyranny in every other quarter of the globe, into the bosom of perfect liberty and freedom in America. Were the great men of the present day, and all those who choose to interfere in public affairs, only to set before them the godlike pleasure of conferring the most lasting and complete state of happiness human nature is capable of, in a state of civil society, on millions yet unborn, and the eternal reward which must attend the doing so much good, I cannot help thinking but contracted views, partial interest, and party factions would sink under, and yield to considerations of so greatly superior a nature.

This sense of a higher destiny, of acting for countless descendants and perhaps for all mankind, gave added dignity to the processes of constitution-making in the Revolutionary era. Generations yet unborn will rise up to honor these men and prove them to have been neither fools, braggarts, nor hypocrites for having exhorted one another to be sensible of the American mission. In the words of an anonymous son of Connecticut who addressed "The Freeborn Sons of America in General" in March, 1776:

It is high time to attend in good earnest to the dictates of common sense, and to be collecting the materials and laying the plan for a more sound Constitution and perfect scheme of Government among ourselves, that will never wax old or decay, nor prove rotten and defective, as all others of human invention have done; but be so wise, permanent, and solid, as to stand in full vigour and glory as long as the sun and moon endureth, and afford to every individual in the present and in all future generations ample security and indemnification of his life, his liberty, and property. Then our peace will be as a river, and our righteousness as the waves of the sea.

Historians have made much of the squabble between radicals and conservatives over legislative-executive relations and the suffrage in the first state constitutions, so much indeed that they have succeeded in concealing the broad agreement among Revolutionary thinkers on constitutional fundamentals. Rare indeed was the American writer who did not concur wholeheartedly with these propositions about the structure and functioning of government:

1) *Whatever the form of government—and there is no one plan good for all men at all times—it should be designed to preserve the maximum liberty and equality of the persons under it.*

In the words of Democraticus, who wrote in 1776 for a Virginia audience:

Political liberty will always be most perfect where the laws have derogated least from the original rights of men, the *rights to equality,* which is adverse to every species of subordination, besides that which arises from the difference of capacity, disposition, and virtue. It is this sense of equality which gives to every man a right to frame and execute his own laws, which alone can secure the observance of justice, and diffuse equal and substantial liberty to the people. . . . It is this principle of equality, this right, which is inherent in every member of the community, to give his own consent to the laws by which he is to be bound, which alone can inspire and preserve the virtue of its members, by placing them in a relation to the publick, and to their fellow citizens, which has a tendency to engage the heart and affections to both. Men love the community in which they are treated with justice, and in which they meet with considerations proportioned to the proofs they give of ability and good intentions. They love those with whom they live on terms of equality, and under a sense of common interests. It engages them in the exercise of their best talents and happiest dispositions, for the government and defence of their country are the best and noblest occupations of men. They lead to the exercise of the greatest virtues and most respectable talents, which is the greatest blessing that any institution can bestow.

Equality in liberty was both more possible and necessary than equality in property. Government should not engage, Samuel Adams warned, in "Utopian schemes of levelling." Rather, wrote an anonymous citizen to the *Boston Gazette*, government must honor an obvious distinction between liberty and property:

Liberty and *Property* are not only join'd in common discourse, but are in their own natures so nearly ally'd, that we cannot be said to possess the one without the enjoyment of the other; and yet there is this distinction to be made between them: All men in their natural and primitive state had an equal right to *possessions*, but when mankind were increased and formed into civil communities, and the whole mass of *property* become unequally divided among them, according to every ones industry and merit, they made laws unanimously for securing each other in their respective acquisitions. Hence it came about, that all men have a right to whatever *property* they can acquire by the laws of a free country; and the principle on which this is founded, is the common good of mankind.

But *liberty*, the source and pillar of all true *property*, cannot be preserved in society while the members possess it unequally. It can no way exist but in its original and native capacity. All men are equally entitled to it. He who assumes more than his just share of *liberty* becomes a tyrant in proportion to what he assumes; and he who loses it becomes so many degrees a slave.

Government should be designed to prevent some men from rising to tyranny and others falling to slavery.

"Liberty, charming liberty," which included the right to pursue happiness, was the central object of the well-planned polity. Liberty was the paramount consideration of the individual, for he had submitted to government primarily to secure it. Liberty was the paramount consideration of the community, because it was, according to a writer in the *Norwich Packet*, "the parent of felicity, of every noble virtue, and even of every art and science." "Liberty effects, and naturally produces Population, Riches, Magnanimity, Arts, Science and Learning,— Trade flows from the same Fountain," wrote another gentleman in Connecticut. More than that, added I. H. in the *Boston News-Letter*, liberty is "the cement of society, and the band of peace, love and unity." In short, a Pennsylvanian echoed:

I take the essential benefit of civil liberty, wheresoever and in whatever degree it is found, to be, its tendency to put in motion and encourage the exertion of all the human powers. It must therefore evidently improve the human mind, and bring with it, in highest perfection, all the advantages of the social state. It is the parent or the nurse of industry, opulence, knowledge, virtue, and heroism.

The makers of constitutions were to keep this one object in view, if necessary to the exclusion of all others: to preserve as much liberty to each man and as much equality among all men as were consistent with the imperatives of a well-ordered society. In practice, of course, this left conservatives and radicals entirely free to haggle over the amount of inequality a well-ordered society demands.

2) *Government should always be "a plain, simple, intelligible thing . . . quite comprehensible by common sense."*

Governments in the past had been made unnecessarily

complicated by elites or tyrants bent on enslaving the mass of the people. "Mysteries of law and government," Samuel Cooke wrote, were "made a cloak of unrighteousness." "Fidelity to the public," to this free and upright people, required that the new laws and constitutions "be as plain and explicit as possible." It required, too, R. H. Lee said, that "every unnecessary power [be] withheld" from government. Although few thinkers except Paine went out of their way to make this point, most would have concurred in a Connecticut author's warning that "No business that can be done by the people themselves should ever be trusted to their Delegates."

The most important step to take toward "plain, simple, intelligible" government was to adopt what Parsons saluted as the only form "consonant to the feelings of the generous and brave Americans . . . a FREE republic." The colonial experience, the events of 1765-1775, and such dramatic assaults on the hereditary system as Paine's *Common Sense* all contributed to the spirit of republicanism in the air in 1776. "Kings and nobles are artificial beings," Salus Populi wrote to "the People of NORTH AMERICA,"

for whose emolument civil society was never intended, and notwithstanding they have had the good fortune to escape general censure from the world, yet I will boldly affirm that nine tenths of all the public calamities which ever befel mankind were brought on by their means. . . .

Mankind never suffered so much during the existence of a republic, as they have suffered in the short reigns of many kings. A Harry VIII did more mischief to his subjects than any republic ever did to its members, notwithstanding that they were so ill constituted. But the true principles of republicanism are at present so well understood, and the mode of conducting such a government so simple and easy, and

America so fit for its reception, that a dozen of wise heads and honest hearts might in one day form a plan for the United Colonies, which would as much excel any one now existing, as the British constitution does that of Caffreria.

Republican government was as good as monarchical or aristocratic government was bad. Phillips Payson explained:

The voice of reason and the voice of God both teach us that the great object or end of government is the public good. Nor is there less certainty in determining that a free and righteous government originates from the people, and is under their direction and control; and therefore a free, popular model of government—of the republican kind—may be judged the most friendly to the rights and liberties of the people, and the most conducive to the public welfare.

By 1776 most American thinkers were quite ready to agree with John Adams that "there is no good government but what is republican."

3) *Government should be kept as near to the people as possible, chiefly through frequent elections and rotation-in-office.*

"All political distinctions ought to be the gift of the free people at large," Salus Populi warned, "and continually to revert to them at the end of the political year, to be renewed or otherwise, as they shall think proper." Agreed, wrote an anonymous publicist to the *Pennsylvania Packet* in 1774, and, what is equally important, "A rotation of offices is one of the lifeguards of liberty." Frequent elections meant, of course, annual elections, and all but one new state constitution made some provision for this method of preserving liberty and equality. Roughly half of them forbade indefinite re-eligibility to the most important executive offices. Most leading thinkers of the period would have praised a New Hampshire author's recipe for freedom:

> An annual, or frequent choice of Magistrates, who in a year, or after a few years, are again left upon a level with their neighbours, is most likely to prevent usurpation and tyranny, and most likely to secure the privileges of the people. If rulers know that they shall, in a short term of time be again out of power, and it may be liable to be called to an account for misconduct, it will guard them against maladministration.

4) *The concept of rulers as servants of the people must be central to all planning for constitutional government.*

This common assumption found expression in the first Virginia and Massachusetts Constitutions:

> All power is vested in, and consequently derived from, the people; magistrates are their trustees and servants, and at all times amenable to them.

> All power residing originally in the people, and being derived from them, the several magistrates and officers of government, vested with authority, whether legislative, executive, or judicial, are their substitutes and agents, and are at all times accountable to them.

"Rulers are no more than attorneys, agents, and trustees, for the people," John Adams wrote, "and if the cause, the interest and trust, is insidiously betrayed, or wantonly trifled away, the people have a right to revoke the authority that they themselves have deputed, and to constitute abler and better agents, attorneys, and trustees." The new state constitutions were full of provisions that expressed or guaranteed this belief.

5) *Government must be constitutional, an empire of*

*laws and not of men: The discretion and whim of all
men in power must be reduced to the lowest level consistent with effective operation of the political machinery.*

The rule of law demanded the existence of a written
constitution, to be acknowledged and administered as a
law superior to the acts of the legislature, decrees of the
judiciary, and ordinances of the executive. Only thus
could liberty be secured against defections of weak rulers
and designs of strong. Said Rev. Stephen Johnson in his
election sermon to the Connecticut legislature:

A good constitution of civil polity, by which, rulers of every
rank and order from the highest to the lowest, hold all their
powers and prerogatives, emoluments and honors; and the
subjects, all their rights and liberties, privileges and immunities; is of very interesting importance to every free state;
without which, all the rights and privileges of subjects, rest
upon a very weak foundation, and are held by a very slippery
and uncertain tenure, the will and caprice of rulers in power.

Rev. Charles Turner expressed much the same idea to
the Massachusetts legislature:

All the wisdom, however, religion and publick spirit, which
have generally existed, or can be expected soon to take place,
among *the great men of the earth*, are by no means a sufficient security to the people, that the end of government will
be honorably answered. Rulers are so prone to have, vastly at
heart, certain worldly interests, inconsistent with the publick
welfare, and the duty they owe to the community, that it is
incumbent on the people (whose right it is to do this, on
proper consideration, and everything else, respecting government, which they judge will be for the salvation and advantage of the whole) to fix on certain regulations, which if we
please we may call a *constitution*, as the standing measure of
the proceedings of government; so determining what powers

they will invest their rulers with, and what privileges they will retain in their own hands.

The written constitution was a major contribution of Revolutionary thinkers and doers—generally the same men—to the development of modern political thought and practice. In one sense, of course, they had no choice in the matter. The colonial heritage, the recent frustrations of defending an unwritten constitution against parliamentary intrusion, the withdrawal of viceregal power and consequent demand for new organs of government—all these factors made the Revolutionary constitutions an inevitable next step in the progress of political liberty. Yet the men of this period deserve credit for insisting, at the very moment of revolution, upon the constructive principle framed by Joseph Warren: "PUBLIC HAPPINESS DEPENDS ON A VIRTUOUS AND UNSHAKEN ATTACHMENT TO A FREE CONSTITUTION." Such popular attachment to a free constitution as higher and controlling law was justified by one, two, or all, of three assumptions: that the constitution was the command of the people, an original compact expressing their unalienable sovereignty; that it was the handiwork of the wisest men in the body politic; that it was an earthly expression of the eternal principles of the law of nature.

Three corollaries of the written constitution are usually traced to or back through this decade of ferment: judicial review, the constitutional convention, and popular ratification. In point of fact, no one of them secured widespread acceptance until some years after 1776. James Otis's memorable harangue in the writs-of-assistance case (1761), the action of a Virginia county court in declaring the Stamp Act unconstitutional, and the general popularity of an American rather than English concept of unconstitutionality were heralds of Hamilton's great effort in *The Federalist*, number 78; but no one was yet so bold or irritated as to assert that the judiciary could refuse to enforce the unconstitutional acts of a representative legislature. Most new state constitutions were written by the provincial legislatures, several of which had some sort of special permission to do this. John Adams and others in theory and Massachusetts in fact (1779) acknowledged that a genuine constitution must be the work of a special convention elected by the people. Likewise, the first formal submission of a draft constitution to a vote of the people took place in Massachusetts in 1778. (And it should be added in passing that the people rejected it.) In general, however, popular election of members of the constitutional convention and popular ratification of their handiwork remained a hope of radical thinkers. Rev. Jonas Clarke of Lexington, a superior political mind, wrote this hope into some town resolutions:

It appears to us that as all government originates from the people; and the great end of government is their peace, safety and happiness; so it is with the people at large, or where that is impracticable, by their Representatives freely and equally elected and empowered for that purpose, to form and agree on a Constitution of government, which being considered and approved by the body of the people, may be enacted, ratified and established.

In May, 1776, the townsmen of Pittsfield, for whom Rev. Thomas Allen served as penman, sent a long memorial to the Massachusetts legislature calling for a new and popular constitution. Several passages in this document merit extended quotation, for they express in earnest fashion the dominant spirit of the time concerning the need of a written constitution, as well as the steadily rising demand for popular participation:

We beg leave, therefore, to represent that we have always been persuaded that the people are the fountain of power; that, since the dissolution of the power of Great Britain over these Colonies, they have fallen into a state of nature.

That the first step to be taken by a people in such a state for the enjoyment or restoration of civil government among them is the formation of a fundamental constitution as the basis and ground-work of legislation. . . .

A representative body may form, but cannot impose said fundamental constitution upon a people, as they, being but servants of the people, cannot be greater than their masters, and must be responsible to them; that, if this fundamental constitution is above the whole legislature, the legislature certainly cannot make it; it must be the approbation of the majority which gives life and being to it; that said fundamental constitution has not been formed for this Province; the corner-stone is not yet laid, and whatever building is reared without a foundation must fall to ruins. . . .

What is the fundamental constitution of this Province? What are the inalienable rights of the people? the power of the rulers? how often to be elected by the people, &c.? Have any of these things been as yet ascertained? Let it not be said by future posterity, that, in this great, this noble, this glorious contest, we made no provision against tyranny among ourselves.

We beg leave to assure your Honors, that . . . *all is to us nothing* while the foundation is unfixed, the corner-stone of government unlaid. We have heard much of government being founded in compact: what compact has been formed as the foundation of government in this Province? We beg leave further to represent, that we have undergone many grievous oppressions in this county, and that now we wish a barrier might be set up against such oppressions, against which we can have no security long till the foundation of government be well established. . . .

Your petitioners, therefore, beg leave to request that this honorable body would form a fundamental constitution for this Province . . . and that said constitution be sent abroad for the approbation of the majority of the people of this Colony; that, in this way, we may emerge from a state of nature, and enjoy again the blessings of civil government.

To this magnificent statement should be added Paine's prophetic burst of eloquence:

But where, say some, is the king of America? I'll tell you, friend, he reigns above, and doth not make havoc of mankind like the Royal Brute of Great Britain. Yet that we may not appear to be defective even in earthly honors, let a day be solemnly set apart for proclaiming the charter; let it be brought forth placed on the divine law, the Word of God; let a crown be placed thereon, by which the world may know, that so far as we approve of monarchy, that in America THE LAW IS KING. For as in absolute governments the king is law, so in free countries the law *ought* to BE king, and there ought to be no other. But lest any ill use should afterwards arise, let the crown at the conclusion of the ceremony be demolished, and scattered among the people whose right it is.

Here, it would seem, in the teachings of a great radical, was the beginning of constitution-worship in America!

TWELVE

TO CONTINUE with the propositions of the American consensus about the structure and functioning of government:

6) *No written constitution can be considered complete unless it embodies a specific declaration of rights.*

Theophilus Parsons made this point repeatedly in his *Essex Result:*

A bill of rights, clearly ascertaining and defining the rights of conscience, and that security of person and property, which every member in the State hath a right to expect from the supreme power thereof, ought to be settled and established, previous to the ratification of any constitution for the State.

Rev. Jonas Clarke expressed the same thought for the people of Lexington:

It appears to us that in emerging from a state of nature into a state of well-regulated society, mankind give up some of their natural rights in order that others of greater importance to their well-being, safety and happiness, both as societies and individuals, might be the better enjoyed, secured and defended. That a civil Constitution or form of government is of the nature of a most sacred covenant or contract entered into by the individuals which form the society, for which such Constitution or form of government is intended, whereby they mutually and solemnly engage to support and defend each other in the enjoyment of those rights which they mean to retain. That the main and great end of establishing any Constitution or form of government among a people or in society, is to maintain, secure and defend those natural rights inviolate. And, consequently, that it is of the highest importance, both to the public peace and utility, and to the safety and security of individuals, that said rights intended to be retained, at least those that are fundamental to the well-being of society and the liberty and safety of individuals, should be in the most explicit terms declared.

The bill of rights was to be something more than a symbol or incantation. The plan and powers of government had to conform to the people's own statement of the rights they were retaining. Maryland, Massachusetts, New Hampshire, North Carolina, Pennsylvania, Vermont, and Virginia all honored this dictate of political liberty in their Revolutionary constitutions. The speed with which a bill of rights emerged from the First Congress is evidence of the strength and persistence of this Revolutionary principle.

7) *A representative legislature is essential to free government.*

We have already noted the central place of the right of representation in Revolutionary thought. We need only recall the primary function of the representative assembly —to serve as the instrument of consent through which the people tax and restrict themselves—to understand why it was the pivot in any and all schemes of government advanced for consideration in this period. For centuries in England, for generations in the colonies, the legislature had been the popular organ of government. It had served the colonists well in the ceaseless campaign against imperial authority, and they had learned to look to it alone for some show of response to their hopes and convictions. Now, with the departure of the royal governor and his retinue, the provincial legislature was not only the essence but the whole of government. This was a condition distasteful, but not yet alarming, to many keen minds. The antics of some of the state legislatures in the first years of independence were to lead in time to the sentiment expressed in Jefferson's *Notes on Virginia*—that "173 despots would surely be as oppressive as one." But in 1776, in theory as in fact, the legislature occupied a dominant position. It was assumed, of course, that American assemblies would observe the four intrinsic limits that Locke had placed upon all legislatures:

These are the bounds which the trust that is put in them by the society and the law of God and Nature have set to the legislative power of every commonwealth, in all forms of government. First: They are to govern by promulgated established laws, not to be varied in particular cases, but to have one rule for rich and poor, for the favourite at Court, and the countryman at plough. Secondly: These laws also ought to be designed for no other end ultimately but the good of the people. Thirdly: They must not raise taxes on the property of the people without the consent of the people given by themselves or their deputies. . . . Fourthly: Legislative neither must nor can transfer the power of making laws to anybody else, or place it anywhere but where the people have.

The framers of several of the first state constitutions inserted provisions in their bills of rights and legislative articles to remind the assembly of these limits so essential to the conduct of government by consent.

8) *A representative legislature is essential to free government, but so, too, are the twin doctrines of the separation of powers and checks and balances.*

A few American writers swung violently in the direction of government by an unrestrained, one-house legislature. A few others clung to a theory of balanced government based on different estates or interests. But most thinkers took a position somewhere between these two extremes, acknowledging both the primacy of the legislature and the necessity for separation and balance. These passages reveal the trend of Revolutionary thinking about the separation of powers and balanced government:

John Adams in a letter to R. H. Lee in 1776:

A legislative, an executive, and a judicial power comprehend the whole of what is meant and understood by government. It is by balancing each of these powers against the other two, that the efforts in human nature towards tyranny can alone be checked and restrained, and any degree of freedom preserved in the constitution.

Article 30 of the Massachusetts Declaration of Rights:

In the government of this commonwealth, the legislative department shall never exercise the executive and judicial powers, or either of them; the executive shall never exercise the legislative and judicial powers, or either of them; the judicial shall never exercise the legislative and executive powers, or either of them, to the end it may be a government of laws and not of men.

Rev. Samuel Cooke to the Massachusetts legislature:

In a civil state, that form is most eligible which is best adapted to promote the ends of government—the benefit of the community. Reason and experience teach that a mixed government is most conducive to this end. In the present imperfect state, the whole power cannot with safety be entrusted with a single person; nor with many, acting jointly in the same public capacity. Various branches of power, concentring in the community from which they originally derive their authority, are a mutual check to each other in their several departments, and jointly secure the common interest. This may indeed, in some instances, retard the operations of government, but will add dignity to its deliberate counsels and weight to its dictates.

C. X. in *Dunlap's Maryland Gazette:*

What is it that constitutes despotism, but the assemblage and union of the legislative, executive, and judicial functions, in the same person, or persons?

Theophilus Parsons in the *Essex Result:*

If the legislative and judicial powers are united, the maker of the law will also interpret it; and the law may then speak a language, dictated by the whims, the caprice, or the prejudice of the judge, with impunity to him— And what people are so unhappy as those, whose laws are uncertain. . . .

Should the executive and legislative powers be united, mischiefs the most terrible would follow. The executive would enact those laws it pleased to execute, and no others— The judicial power would be set aside as inconvenient and tardy— The security and protection of the subject would be a shadow — The executive power would make itself absolute, and the government end in a tyranny. . . .

Should the executive and judicial powers be united, the subject would then have no permanent security of his person and property. The executive power would interpret the laws and bend them to his will; and, as he is the judge, he may leap over them by artful construction, and gratify, with impunity, the most rapacious passions. . . . Indeed the dependence of any of these powers upon either of the others, which in all states has always been attempted by one or the other of them, has so often been productive of such calamities, and of the shedding of such oceans of blood, that the page of history seems to be one continued tale of human wretchedness.

Here, in the words of framers and critics of the first constitutions, are the major considerations that impelled them to choose divided and balanced government. Their central object, of course, was human liberty. Whatever ends mixed government had served in the past, such as to represent different estates or interests in the community, its prime purpose now was to divide the totality of governmental power into separate portions, to be exercised by separate organs under a system of restraints held in delicate balance. Only one estate or interest could be recognized in a free constitution—that of all the people voluntarily associated in the commonwealth. It was their power that each branch exercised, their interest that each represented. The separation of powers was something of a retreat from the principle that government should be "a plain, simple, intelligible thing." A unified government would certainly be easier to run and understand. Yet the advantages to be gained from separation and balance far outweighed those to be gained from union. Liberty rather than authority, protection rather than power, delay rather than efficiency were the concern of these constitution-makers. Unrestrained government had led to their distress, and unrestrained government, even by their own representatives, was not to be countenanced again. Once again the Revolutionists drew upon the Anglo-American past in a selective way, and once again the criterion of choice was their passion for liberty. Whatever the difficulties of balanced government, such a system was "essential to Liberty."

9) *Government in a free state is properly the concern of all those who have "a common interest with, and an attachment to the community." The right to vote, as well as to hold office, should be limited to men who have an evident "stake-in-society"—first, because they alone can make competent, responsible, uncorrupted judgments; second, because they alone have a clear right to consent to laws regulating or restricting the use of property.*

The appeal of the principle of natural equality was not strong enough at this time to overcome inherited traditions and prejudices. Few voices were raised for universal suffrage, even universal white male suffrage. Only in leveling Vermont, as portent of things to come, was the traditional property qualification abandoned without reserve. The men who wrote the other state constitutions restricted political participation to those who held property or paid taxes. In so doing, they remained true to a fundamental political principle of the colonial period, a principle expressed by Nathaniel Ames in his almanac for 1774: "Law in a free country is or ought to be the determination of those who have property in land."

By this time, of course, the growth of trade and cities had brought political recognition to other types of property. Out of a wide variety of qualifications for suffrage in the new constitutions, these may be noted as representative of different shades of emphasis within the area of general agreement: in conservative South Carolina, "a freehold at least of fifty acres of land, or a town lot," or equivalent property; in conservative Maryland, "real or personal property above the value of five hundred pounds current money"; in middle-of-the-road Massachusetts, "a freehold estate" with an "annual income of three pounds, or any estate of the value of sixty pounds"; in liberal Pennsylvania, mere payment of "public taxes." In the more conservative states these provisions were backed up by other provisions limiting office-holding to men of property. The oligarchs of South Carolina pushed this practice to the limit in setting this qualification for governor or councilor: "a settled plantation or freehold . . . of the value of at least ten thousand pounds currency, clear of debt."

It is surprising how small an output of theory seemed necessary to justify this practice. One of the few men to face this question squarely was Theophilus Parsons, who answered it thus in the *Essex Result:*

The only objects of legislation . . . are the person and property of the individuals which compose the state. If the law affects only the persons of the members, the consent of a majority of any members is sufficient. If the law affects the property only, the consent of those who hold a majority of the property is enough. If it affects, (as it will very frequently, if not always,) both the person and property, the consent of a majority of the members, and of those members also who hold a majority of the property, is necessary. If the consent of the latter is not obtained, their interest is taken from them against their consent, and their boasted security of property is vanished. Those who make the law, in this case give and grant what is not theirs. . . .

If each member, without regard to his property, has equal influence in legislation with any other, it follows, that some members enjoy greater benefits and powers in legislation than others, when these benefits and powers are compared with the rights parted with to purchase them. For the property-holder parts with the controul over his person, as well as he who hath no property, and the former also parts with the controul over his property, of which the latter is destitute. Therefore to constitute a perfect law in a free state, affecting the persons and property of the members, it is necessary that the law be for the good of the whole, which is to be determined by a majority of the members, and that majority should include those, who possess a major part of the property in the state.

Actually, Parsons was more advanced than most men in his ideas about representation of persons. So, too, was Joseph Hawley, who argued for the town of Northampton that the upper house should represent property and the lower house persons. Most writers simply remained silent on this question, for the stake-in-society principle seemed too essential a part of ordered liberty to require justification or merit indignation. It was left to the next two generations to search this problem exhaustively. The men of the Revolution were sure that this was one of those instances in which natural equality should give way to an obvious imperative of the well-ordered society. Property qualifications for office-holding were justified on the same general principle: the importance of a citizenry attached by more than accident of birth to the common weal. Fifty acres of land or an income of three pounds were evidence of such attachment. The plea of a New Hampshire radical —"Let it not be said in future generations that money was made by the founders of the American States an essential qualification in the rulers of a free people"—was considered premature and demagogic. Any man worth his salt could get fifty acres or earn three pounds.

Parsons was also one of the few men to consider the

problem of women's suffrage, which he disposed of neatly in this solemn passage:

> Women what age soever they are of, are . . . considered as not having a sufficient acquired discretion; not from a deficiency in their mental powers, but from the natural tendency and delicacy of their minds, their retired mode of life, and various domestic duties. These concurring, prevent that promiscuous intercourse with the world, which is necessary to qualify them for electors.

Hawley agreed that Parsons had handled this problem "very sensibly, as well as genteely," all of which proves that words are what each generation makes them.

Within the broad area of patriot consensus we have already noted several sharp differences of opinion. We may conclude these two chapters with an ordered review of the disputes that enlivened the writing of the new state constitutions. For the most part, these disputes were political rather than theoretical in nature and are therefore not properly the concern of this discussion. Conservatives and radicals who struggled for supremacy in states like Pennsylvania and Maryland agreed with few exceptions on such fundamental points as republicanism, a strong legislature, declarations of rights, the separation of powers, and property qualifications. The differences between them, irreconcilable as they must have seemed at the time, were the differences of men who spoke the same political language:

First, conservatives emphasized divided and balanced government, radicals held out for legislative dominance. All insisted on an executive branch separate from the legislature, but fell out over questions of tenure, number, independence, qualifications, powers, and mode of election. Conservatives tended to favor the type of executive outlined in the New York Constitution of 1777 and the Massachusetts Constitution of 1780. Radicals showed what they had in mind in the Pennsylvania, North Carolina, and New Hampshire constitutions. The manner in which selective emphasis on different points in a common and not wholly symmetrical political theory can lead to a bitter clash of opinions was also illustrated in the problem of the judiciary. Few radicals could take pleasure in John Adams's prescription for an independent judiciary: appointment by governor and council, tenure "for life," salaries "ascertained and established by law."

Second, conservatives considered the doctrine of popular sovereignty a useful notion that was not to be applied too literally in concrete situations. Radicals were inclined to accept popular sovereignty at face value. A consistent radical thinker, a man who was of course not easy to find, favored male taxpayer suffrage, popular participation in framing and ratifying constitutions, no property qualifications for office-holding, a popularly elected governor (if to be elected by a source other than the legislature), and annual elections for all offices. A consistent conservative, perhaps a little easier to unearth, pushed for high property qualifications for voting, even higher qualifications for office-holding, appointments to office, and longer terms.

Finally, the whole emphasis of the conservative was placed on government more complicated, delaying, "high-toned" than that simple scheme fixed in the minds of democrats like Franklin and Paine. The healthy difference of opinion between unicameralists and bicameralists is perhaps the most instructive case in point. To the argument of the former that the scheme of two houses was "a feudal relict," "a source of trouble," and "a step towards arbitrary power," Parsons made answer:

> But the legislative power must not be trusted with one assembly. A single assembly is frequently influenced by the vices, follies, passions, and prejudices of an individual. It is liable to be avaricious, and to exempt itself from the burdens it lays upon it's constituents. It is subject to ambition, and after a series of years, will be prompted to vote itself perpetual. . . .
>
> The result of a single assembly will be hasty and indigested, and their judgments frequently absurd and inconsistent. There must be a second body to revise with coolness and wisdom, and to controul with firmness, independent upon the first, either for their creation, or existence. Yet the first must retain a right to a similar revision and controul over the second.

Supporters of unicameralism achieved their only constitutional successes in Pennsylvania, Georgia, and Vermont, and many of them lived to regret it.

The struggle for political supremacy in each of the new states was accompanied by violent literary debate over the structure, authority, and basis of government. The distance between conservative and radical in Pennsylvania or South Carolina, or between Carter Braxton's *Address to the Convention . . . of Virginia* and the anonymous New Hampshire tract *The People the Best Governors*, was enormous, yet it was the distance between men who stood at opposite edges of a broad, unbroken plateau. Each could look back over his shoulder at the great mass of patriots, perhaps nine in ten of whom were in accord on fundamentals of constitutional theory. At the center of the plateau and of the people who stood upon it was John

Adams of Massachusetts. His little pamphlet *Thoughts on Government*, published in Philadelphia and Boston in 1776, was the most lucid, moderate, representative statement of the theory of ordered liberty out of which the best of the new constitutions arose. And its message about the structure of government was simply this: The great ends of the political community, the liberty and happiness of the men who have created it, will be most successfully answered by government that is limited, divided, balanced, representative, republican, responsible, and constitutional.

We must not overstate the success or originality of the Revolutionary constitutions. Several of them created governments that oscillated violently between anarchy and tyranny; others were little better than a mask for the oligarchy of the "eastern bashaws." The failure of such innovations as Pennsylvania's fantastic Council of Censors leads straight to the judgment that the more faithfully the patriots modeled their new governments on colonial precedents, the more success they achieved as constitution-makers. Yet this period of trial-and-error, which was also, be it remembered, a period of war and desolation, was a necessary prelude to the triumph of republican government under Washington, Adams, and Jefferson. As the second of these men wrote of the state constitutions in 1787:

The United States of America have exhibited, perhaps, the first example of governments erected on the simple principles of nature; and if men are now sufficiently enlightened to disabuse themselves of artifice, imposture, hypocrisy, and superstition, they will consider this event as an era in their history. . . . Thirteen governments . . . founded on the natural authority of the people alone, without a pretence of miracle or mystery, and which are destined to spread over the northern part of that whole quarter of the globe, are a great point gained in favor of the rights of mankind. The experiment is made, and has completely succeeded; it can no longer be called in question, whether authority in magistrates and obedience of citizens can be grounded on reason, morality, and the Christian religion, without the monkery of priests, or the knavery of politicians.

THIRTEEN

The Moral Basis of Government

HOWEVER ANGRILY they might argue over points of constitutional structure, the American spokesmen agreed unanimously that it would take more than a perfect plan of government to preserve ordered liberty. Something else was needed, some moral principle diffused among the people to strengthen the urge to peaceful obedience and hold the community on an even keel. The wisest of political philosophers had spoken of three possibilities: fear, honor, virtue. Which were Americans to choose?

The answer, of course, was virtue, for as the author of *The People the Best Governors* observed (in a direct steal from Montesquieu), "Fear is the principle of a despotic, honour of a kingly, and virtue is the principle of a republican government." "The spirit of a free republican constitution, or the moving power which should give it action," Theophilus Parsons wrote at the end of his great *Essex Result,* "ought to be political virtue, patriotism, and a just regard to the natural rights of mankind." And Samuel Adams spoke for all American thinkers when he reminded James Warren:

We may look up to Armies for our Defence, but Virtue is our best Security. It is not possible that any State sh[d] long remain free, where Virtue is not supremely honord.

"Liberty cannot be preserved," another Bostonian added, "if the manners of the people are corrupted, nor absolute monarchy introduced, where they are sincere." Free government rested on a definite moral basis: a virtuous people. Conversely, the decay of a people's morals signaled the end of liberty and happiness. On no point in the whole range of political theory were Americans more thoroughly in accord. Free government was in large part a problem in practical ethics.

Revolutionary thinkers drew heavily on their colonial heritage in proclaiming virtue the essence of freedom. The decade of crisis brought new popularity to the cult of virtue that had long held sway in the colonies. All the familiar techniques that earlier colonists had borrowed from England and converted to their purposes were revived for the emergency. The appeal to ancient Rome for republican inspiration was especially favored. The nicest compliment Samuel Adams could pay Joseph Hawley was to say that he had "as much of the stern Virtue and Spirit of a Roman Censor as any Gentleman I ever conversed with." John Dickinson had spoken "with Attick Eloquence and Roman Spirit"; the dead of Concord were "like the Romans of old"; the way to exhort the Americans was to "stir up all that's Roman in them." The Roman example worked both ways: From the decline of the republic Americans could learn the fate of free states that succumb to luxury. The colonists' own ancestors proved equally useful. Thousands of farmers read in Nathaniel Ames's almanac for 1769:

> When our Forefathers firm maintain'd the cause
> Of true Religion, Liberty and Laws,
> Disdaining down the golden Stream to glide,
> But bravely stem'd Corruptions rapid Tide,
> Shall we, by Indolence, supinely doom
> To Sweat and Toil the Nations yet to come?

The praise of virtue and condemnation of corruption served two very practical purposes in the decade that led to 1776: to mobilize public opinion as sanction for various extra-legal associations and governments, and to tear men loose from their traditional deference to all things British. Most of the ceaseless preaching about "the fatal effects of luxury to a free state" was directed at the mother country. This was especially true in the last months before independence, when men like Edward Bancroft began to argue that the "Effeminacy, Luxury, and Corruption, which extend to all Orders of Men" in England would poison the youthful body of America unless it were to cut short its dependence. "Americans!" exclaimed one writer in March, 1776,

> Remember the long, habitual, base venality of *British* Parliaments.
> Remember the corrupt, putrefied state of that nation, and the virtuous, sound, healthy, state of your own young constitution.
> Remember the tyranny of *Mezentius*, who bound living men face to face with dead ones, and the effect of it.

And Caractacus wrote to the *Pennsylvania Packet*:

> We thrived upon her wholesome milk during our infancy. She then enjoyed a sound constitution. I will not say that it is high time we should be taken from her breasts, but I will say, that she has played the harlot in her old age, and that if we

continue to press them too closely we shall extract nothing from them but disease and death.

To a British officer's sneer that "the People of America are at least an hundred Years behind the old Countries in Refinement," An American replied in the New London *Connecticut Gazette*:

As to Humanity, Temperance, Chastity, Justice, a Veneration for the Rights of Mankind, and every Moral Virtue, they are an hundred years behind us.

This, of course, was why Americans could launch a republic with some hope of success, for it was the one form of government, John Adams pointed out, "whose principle and foundation is virtue."

In the process of exhorting one another to be brave, frugal, and honest, and of damning England as "that degen'rate land," American writers worked out a well-rounded theory of the ethical basis of free government. In particular, they identified the essential public virtues, described the contrasting political fates of good men and bad, and recommended techniques for promoting virtue and discouraging vice.

In addition to approving all recognized Christian, Roman, and English virtues, Americans singled out several attitudes or traits of special consequence for a free republic: first, the willingness to act morally without compulsion, to obey the laws of nature as interpreted by reason and the laws of man as established in consent; second, the love of liberty, the desire for the adventure and sacrifices of free government rather than the false security of tyranny; third, public spirit and patriotism, defined by A Native in 1776 for the enlightenment of his fellow Virginians as "a disinterested attachment to the publick good, exclusive and independent of all private and selfish interest"; fourth, official incorruptibility, a state of virtue saluted by Jefferson in the *Summary View* when he reminded George III that "the whole art of government consists in the art of being honest"; and fifth, industry and frugality, hard work and plain living, the only path to personal liberty and national independence. Special attention was devoted to the fifth of these qualities, for industry and frugality were essential to the success of America's program of economic resistance. The uproar over industry and frugality, private no less than public virtues, reached such a pitch in New England as to call forth this reminder from A Freeholder in the *New-Hampshire Gazette*:

Whilst Frugality and Industry are strongly recommended at this Juncture of Time, I think Cleanliness in our public Ways and Streets may not be an Object unworthy of our particular Attention.

Whether cleanliness, too, was essential to liberty was never made clear in Revolutionary literature, but the cultivation of these great public virtues—moral action without compulsion, love of liberty, public spirit, incorruptibility, and industry and frugality—was considered the first duty of a free people. Men who displayed these qualities were the raw materials of liberty. Without such men, in low places as well as high, free government could not possibly exist.

The fruits of virtue, for nations as well as men, were liberty, prosperity, and happiness; the fruits of corruption and luxury were tyranny, poverty, and misery. "The peculiar blessings of heaven," Rev. Thomas Coombe wrote in 1775, "do indeed seem generally to be the reward of DETERMINED VIRTUE in a people." "And as too great authority intoxicates and poisons Kings," Nathaniel Ames warned, "so luxury poisons a whole nation." True, echoed Rev. Phillips Payson, and the upshot is this:

The baneful effects of exorbitant wealth, the lust of power, and other evil passions, are so inimical to a free, righteous government, and find such an easy access to the human mind, that it is difficult, if possible, to keep up the spirit of good government.

How to encourage virtue and thus "keep up the spirit of good government"? To this key question of political liberty Americans replied: hortatory religion, sound education, honest government, and a simple economy.

The strain of piety in the philosophy of American liberty is evident in the appeal of the Declaration of Independence to "Nature's God," the "Creator," and "the Supreme Judge of the World." Few thinking laymen, whether believers like Samuel Adams or skeptics like Franklin, ever doubted the indispensability of organized religion in the preservation of public and private morality. The former wrote to his friend John Scollay:

I fully agree in Opinion with a very celebrated Author, that "Freedom or Slavery will prevail in a (City or) Country according as the Disposition & Manners of the People render them fit for the one or the other"; and I have long been convinced that our Enemies have made it an Object, to eradicate from the Minds of the People in general a Sense of true Religion & Virtue, in hopes thereby the more easily to carry their Point of enslaving them. Indeed my Friend, this is a Subject so important in my Mind, that I know not how to leave it. Revelation assures us that "Righteousness exalteth a Nation"—Communities are dealt with in this World by the wise and just Ruler of the Universe. He rewards or punishes them according to their general Character. The diminution of publick Virtue is usually attended with that of publick Happiness, and the publick Liberty will not long survive the total Extinction of Morals.

Patriot preachers, of course, found this a favorite theme. The practice of the Christian religion was as essential to virtue as was the practice of virtue to freedom. "Survey the globe," Rev. John Joachim Zubly urged, "and you will find that liberty has taken its seat only in Christendom, and that the highest degree of freedom is pleaded for and enjoyed by such as make profession of the gospel." Rev. Phillips Payson put the case for religion to the Massachusetts legislature in these blunt words:

The importance of religion to civil society and government is great indeed, as it keeps alive the best sense of moral obligation, a matter of such extensive utility, especially in respect to an oath, which is one of the principal instruments of government. The fear and reverence of God, and the terrors of eternity, are the most powerful restraints upon the minds of men; and hence it is of special importance in a free government, the spirit of which being always friendly to the sacred rights of conscience, it will hold up the gospel as the great rule of faith and practice. . . . The thoughtful and wise among us trust that our civil fathers, from a regard to gospel worship and the constitution of these churches, will carefully preserve them, and at all times guard against every innovation that might tend to overset the public worship of God, though such innovations may be urged from the most foaming zeal. . . . Let the restraints of religion once be broken down . . . and we might well defy all human wisdom and power to support and preserve order and government in the state. Human conduct and character can never be better formed than upon the principles of our holy religion; they give the justest sense, the most adequate views, of the duties between rulers and people.

In short, religion helped put the order in ordered liberty, especially by emphasizing the dependence of public morality on private virtue. The Massachusetts Convention of 1779 responded to this sort of exhortation by inserting these words in the Declaration of Rights:

As the happiness of a people, and the good order and preservation of a civil government, essentially depend upon piety, religion, and morality; and as these cannot be generally diffused through a community, but by the institution of the public worship of GOD, and of public instruction in piety, religion, and morality—therefore, to promote their happiness, and to secure the good order and preservation of their government, the people of this commonwealth have a right to invest their legislature with power to authorize and require, and the legislature shall, from time to time, authorize and require the several towns, parishes, precincts, and other bodies politic or religious societies, to make suitable provision, at their own expense, for the institution of the public worship of God, and for the support and maintenance of public Protestant teachers of piety, religion, and morality, in all cases where such provision shall not be made voluntarily.

The doctrine of religious necessity had not yet given way to the doctrine of full religious liberty.

The second means of promoting virtue was public and private education. Like their colonial forebears, the men of the Revolution considered the inculcation of morality one of the three or four basic purposes of all instruments of education. Said Rev. Simeon Howard:

Liberty and learning are so friendly to each other, and so naturally thrive and flourish together, that we may justly expect that the guardians of the former will not neglect the latter. The good education of children is a matter of great importance to the commonwealth. Youth is the time to plant the mind with the principles of virtue, truth and honour, the love of liberty and of their country, and to furnish it with all useful knowledge; and though in this business much depends upon parents, guardians, and masters, yet it is incumbent upon the government to make provision for schools and all suitable means of instruction.

Natural law and virtue were closely identified in the Revolutionary mind. Since God and nature told men not only what they had a right to do, but what was right for them to do, the practice of virtue was simply obedience to natural law. It was the business of educators and ministers to instruct their charges that the fairest right of all was to do what was right, that true liberty was the liberty to follow God's plan for human happiness. John Winthrop had expressed exactly the same idea in defense of theocratic oligarchy, but John Winthrop's God had long since mellowed.

I have already quoted John Adams's hope that colleges would be "instruments of impressing on the tender mind, and of spreading and distributing far and wide, the ideas of right and the sensations of freedom." Fourteen years later he drafted this clause of the Massachusetts Constitution of 1780:

Wisdom and knowledge, as well as virtue, diffused generally among the body of the people, being necessary for the preservation of their rights and liberties, and as these depend on spreading the opportunities and advantages of education in the various parts of the country, and among the different orders of the people, it shall be the duty of legislators and magistrates, in all future periods of this commonwealth, to cherish the interests of literature and the sciences, and all seminaries of them; especially the university at Cambridge, public schools and grammar schools in the towns; to encourage private societies and public institutions, rewards and immunities for the promotion of agriculture, arts, sciences, commerce, trades, manufactures, and a natural history of the country; to countenance and inculcate the principles of humanity and general benevolence, public and private charity, industry and frugality, honesty and punctuality in their dealings, sincerity, good humor, and all social affections and generous sentiments among the people.

The two passages just quoted from the Massachusetts Constitution indicate something of the importance of government as a promoter of virtue. Not only did it nourish morality indirectly by encouraging and protecting, and perhaps supporting, the instruments of religion and education; it was expected to make a number of direct contributions: by passing sumptuary laws "to discourage prodigality and extravagance, vain and expensive amusements and fantastic foppery, and to encourage the opposite virtues"; by making proclamations from time to time of days "of public humiliation, fasting and prayer"; and by itself operating at the highest level of justice, virtue, and incorruptibility. Preachers never tired of exhorting legislators and judges to be men of spotless integrity in both public and private dealings. Orators never tired of reminding the public that it should look for virtue before all other qualities in selecting candidates for public office.

Finally, one influential group of Revolutionary thinkers asserted that the virtues necessary to maintain free government were more likely to flourish in an agrarian than in a manufacturing or commercial economy. "Would you extinguish luxury?" asked a South Carolinian in 1773.

"Give a singular protection to agriculture, which engages men to live in temperance and frugality." A Connecticut gentleman quoted Pitt in 1775 on the importance to freedom of "the proprietors, and tillers of the ground—men who have a permanent, natural right in the place—and who from being nursed in the bosom of cultivation, form strong and honorable attachments to their country." And Josiah Quincy, Jr., saluted "the FREEHOLDERS and YEOMANRY of my country . . . the LANDED INTEREST" as "the virtue, strength, and fortitude" of the state. The strong agrarian bias of Jeffersonian democracy had roots in the colonial and Revolutionary past.

American writers stressed the interdependence of virtue and each of these forces. Just as religion, education, government, and agriculture could raise the level of public and private morality, so morality could strengthen each of these great human undertakings. This was especially true of morality and government. Virtue fed liberty, liberty fed virtue. More to the point, John Adams wrote, vice brought tyranny, which in turn brought more vice:

Obsta principiis, nip the shoots of arbitrary power in the bud, is the only maxim which can ever preserve the liberties of any people. When the people give way, their deceivers, betrayers, and destroyers press upon them so fast, that there is no resisting afterwards. The nature of the encroachment upon the American constitution is such, as to grow every day more and more encroaching. Like a cancer, it eats faster and faster every hour. The revenue creates pensioners, and the pensioners urge for more revenue. The people grow less steady, spirited, and virtuous, the seekers more numerous and more corrupt, and every day increases the circles of their dependents and expectants, until virtue, integrity, public spirit, simplicity, and frugality, become the objects of ridicule and scorn, and vanity, luxury, foppery, selfishness, meanness, and downright venality swallow up the whole society.

The business of political philosophers was to discover the virtues that lead to free government and the form of government that leads men to virtue. In fact, said Americans like Nathaniel Ames, expressing an opinion more than two thousand years old, that form of government is best which produces the greatest number of good, free, happy men. The colonies had enough virtue to be republics, and as republics they could look forward to an increase in virtue. David Ramsay explained it all on the second anniversary of independence:

Our present form of government is every way preferable to the royal one we have lately renounced. It is much more favorable to purity of morals, and better calculated to promote all our important interests. Honesty, plain-dealing, and simple manners, were never made the patterns of courtly behavior. Artificial manners always prevail in kingly government; and royal courts are reservoirs, from whence insincerity, hypocrisy, dissimulation, pride, luxury, and extravagance, deluge and overwhelm the body of the people. On the other hand, republics are favorable to truth, sincerity, frugality, industry, and simplicity of manners. Equality, the life and soul of commonwealth, cuts off all pretensions to preferment, but those which arise from extraordinary merit.

Whether this youthful, virtuous people would lose its virtue with its youth and its freedom with its virtue was a question much debated by thoughtful Americans. Young John Adams could write:

If ever an infant country deserved to be cherished it is America. If ever any people merited honor and happiness they are her inhabitants. They are a people whom no character can flatter or transmit in any expressions equal to their merit and virtue; with the high sentiments of Romans, in the most prosperous and virtuous times of that commonwealth, they have the tender feelings of humanity and the noble benevolence of Christians; they have the most habitual, radical sense of liberty, and the highest reverence for virtue; they are descended from a race of heroes, who, placing their confidence in Providence alone, set the seas and skies, monsters and savages, tyrants and devils, at defiance for the sake of religion and liberty.

But young Theophilus Parsons could ask:

The most virtuous states have become vicious. The morals of all people, in all ages, have been shockingly corrupted. . . . Shall we alone boast an exemption from the general fate of mankind? Are our private and political virtues to be transmitted untainted from generation to generation, through a course of ages?

Two things were certain: First, the end of virtue and liberty would come by easy stages rather than in one grand cataclysm. "History does not more clearly point out any fact than this," warned Richard Henry Lee, "that nations which have lapsed from liberty, to a state of slavish subjection, have been brought to this unhappy condition, by gradual paces." Eternal vigilance was the price of virtue as well as liberty. Second, should Americans sink from virtue and liberty to vice and slavery, they would have only themselves to blame. It was clearly in their power to build and preserve a free republic. Rev. Samuel Webster of Salisbury, delivering the Massachusetts election sermon for 1777, laid down eleven commandments for a people determined to be free:

1. Let the people by all means encourage *schools* and *colleges,* and all the means of *learning* and *knowledge,* if

they would guard against *slavery*. For a *wise*, a *knowing* and a *learned* people, are the least likely of any in the world to be enslaved.

2. Let them do all in their power to *suppress* vice and *promote religion* and *virtue*. For, besides their *natural* efficacy, I am persuaded no people were ever yet given up by God to *slavery*, till they had first given themselves up to *wickedness*.

3. Let only men of *integrity* be entrusted by you with any *power*. I think power is much safer in their hands than in men of *greater abilities*, but who are wanting in this essential point.

4. Let not *too much power* be trusted in the hands of any. It may hurt them, and then they may hurt the public. Or if it seem necessary in some critical time (like the present) to lodge great power in some *hand* or hands, let it be for a *limited time*, and the power renewed *annually*, if there is occasion.

5. Let elections of the *Legislators* be *frequent*; and let *bribery* and *corruption* be guarded against to the utmost. Methinks, those who are guilty of these should be forever rendered incapable of any place of *power* or *trust*; and this by a fundamental law of the constitution.

6. Let the *militia* be kept under the best regulation, and be made *respectable*. This will be a great security a great many ways.

7. Let *standing armies* be only for *necessity* and for a *limited time*. For, when corrupted, they have been the ruin of many a country's *liberty*.

8. Let these *armies* never be put under the absolute power of any magistrate in time of peace, so as to act in any *cause*, till that *cause* is approved by the *Senate* and *people*.

9. Let *monopolies* and all *kinds* and degrees of *oppression* be carefully guarded against. They are dangerous to the *peace* of a *people*, and they are dangerous to their *liberties!* I am mistaken if the present time does not prove it.

10. Let a *careful watch* be kept, and if any is found

grossly and *notoriously* exceeding the *limits* of his power, me-thinks, it should be a standing invariable rule never to trust him with any power more.

Finally, let the *powers* and *prerogatives* of the *rulers* and the *rights* and *priviledges* of the people, be determined with as much precision as possible, that all may know their limits. And where there is any dispute, *let nothing be done*, till it is settled by the people, who are the fountain of power.

This was an almost perfect statement of the American consensus on the moral basis of government and how to stiffen it.

Conclusion

CONSERVATISM, we are told, is the worship of dead revolutionists. If this is true, then Americans are conservatives twice over. Not only do we worship long-dead revolutionists, responding with religious fervor to the cadences of the great Declaration in which they appealed to a candid world; the Revolution itself was as respectful of the past as a genuine revolution can be. Not only does our political faith stem directly from that of the American Revolution; the latter reached back through the colonial past almost to the beginning of Western political thought. The Americans of 1776 were the first men in modern history to defend rather than seek an open society and constitutional liberty; their political faith, like the appeal to arms it supported, was therefore surprisingly sober.

It would seem useful to end this journey through early American thought by summing up the faith that guided the minds and raised the spirits of the Revolutionists. We must again recall that the Revolution produced neither a universal thinker nor a definitive book. The political thought of this great crisis was a popular creed that hundreds of gifted, hopeful leaders shouted in the midst of combat and tens of thousands of less gifted but no less hopeful followers took to their hearts. But if one able Revolutionist had set himself consciously to express the political consensus of his time, to cast the principles of 1776 in a pattern for later ages to ponder, this might well have been the outline he would have chosen to follow— this was the political thought of the American Revolution:

I. The political and social world is governed by laws as certain and universal as those which govern the physical world. Whether these laws are direct commands of God, necessities of nature, or simply inescapable lessons of history makes little practical difference. In any or all of these cases, men are guided and restricted by a moral order that they may defy but cannot alter. Reason and experience, the means through which men come to understand these laws, point out at least four instances in which they are applicable to the affairs of men. The higher law, or law of nature, is all these things:

1. A set of moral standards governing private conduct: The law of nature commands men to love, assist, and respect one another and to live godly, righteous, and sober lives.

2. A system of abstract justice to which the laws of men should conform: No human laws are of any validity if contrary to the laws of nature. In practice, this means that positive law which runs counter to a community's inherited sense of right and wrong is not only bad-law but no law at all.

3. A line of demarcation around the proper sphere of political authority: A government that pushes beyond it into forbidden fields does so at peril of resistance or even revolution. Government must obey the commands of natural law or release men from obedience.

4. The source of natural rights, those rights which belong to man as man: From the law of nature flow man's rights to life, liberty, property, conscience, and happiness. The law of nature wills that men be free and happy.

The law of nature is a call to moral action on the part of men as individuals and the community as their servant. To men and nations who obey this law come prosperity and happiness; to men and nations who defy it come adversity and sadness. History has a way of punishing those who deny the reality of moral restraints on political power.

II. Since men are the raw materials out of which the community is constructed, the nature of man is the key to all major questions of political power and organization. The nature of man is such as to make free government possible but far from inevitable. He is by no means so good and perfectible as one line of philosophers insists; he is by no means so evil or degenerate as another line would have it. He dwells at a moral level considerably lower than that inhabited by angels, yet surely he is something more than a beast walking upright. Man is a composite of good and evil, of ennobling excellencies and degrading imperfections.

The most politically significant of his "good" qualities are sociability, love of liberty, basic human decency, and reasonableness. The first of these—the impulse to associate and co-operate with other men in pursuit of common ends —is unquestionably the most influential. So strong is the urge man feels to live and work with other men that he may properly be considered a political and social animal. The famous "state of nature" is at best a logical hypothesis. Man has no choice, thanks to his own nature, except to be in society and under government.

The most politically significant of his "bad" qualities are

selfishness, depravity, passion, moral laziness, and corruptibility. The last of these—the lust for power and the inability to withstand its corrupting effects—is the one vice
that constitution-makers must keep constantly in mind.
The discretion left to rulers and the duration of their
terms of office must each be reduced to the lowest level
compatible with the need for effective government.

If man is a composite of good and evil, then one of the
chief ends of the community is to separate his vices from
his virtues and help him pursue his better nature. True
religion, constitutional government, and sound education
are the leading types of collective action that can help
him to do this. The first of these encourages man to suppress his savage impulses; the second forces him to think
before acting; the third teaches him the delights of virtue
and liberty and the sorrows of vice and slavery. In short,
man's saving grace, at least for earthly purposes, is his
capacity for learning. While different men can acquire
knowledge in different amounts, any man can acquire the
minimum necessary for survival and citizenship. It is
therefore the business of government to encourage the
means of general education.

III. If the natural character of man is an alloy of virtue
and vice, his natural state is pure freedom and equality.
Men may be grossly unequal in appearance, talents, intelligence, virtue, and fortune, but to this extent at least
they are absolutely equal: No man has any natural right
of dominion over any other; every man is free in the sight
of God and plan of nature. This eternal principle of natural equality is not incompatible with political, social, or
economic stratification, but the burden of proof rests
squarely upon advocates of artificial inequality: It is for
them to demonstrate that an unequal arrangement is es-

sential to the stability, prosperity, or independence of the community. Conversely, the goal of political science is to discover a scheme of government that will reduce inequalities without invading individual liberty or menacing the welfare and security of the community.

IV. All men have certain fundamental rights. These rights are natural, traceable directly to the great plan of nature, if not indeed to God; absolute, belonging to men before, outside of, and quite without regard to organized government or society; eternal, never varying in content or identity; essential, since necessary to man's existence as man; and unalienable, impossible to be surrendered either absolutely or permanently. Five rights are clearly of this transcendent character: the right to life, which carries with it the power of self-preservation; the right to liberty, to act as one pleases without external restraint or control of any earthly sort; the right to property, to use and dispose of the fruits of honest industry; the right to happiness, or at least to pursue it on equal terms with other men; and the right to a free conscience, to reach out for God without interference or even assistance.

V. Although the natural rights of man are unalienable and can never be surrendered to any earthly authority, men can surrender their original power to control the exercise of these rights. They do this through a process of free consent in which they give away a certain amount of this power in return for the protection of the community. Just how much of this power they can and should surrender is a key question of political theory. Every man must surrender enough control over his original rights to permit government to maintain an organized, stable, peaceful pattern of human relations. No man should surrender so much that government dictates his every action. Between these two self-evident extremes the balance of liberty and authority must ever be in constant motion. In a free state the balance tips decisively in the direction of liberty. Men in such a state are generally virtuous; they make a conscious effort to use their freedom and property in a way that does not interfere with the freedom and property of the men with whom they must live and do business. Government intervention is the exception rather than the rule. In autocratic states, where men are usually ignorant and immoral, the balance tips just as decisively toward authority. Government is arbitrary because men will not respect one another. The balance between liberty and authority in any particular community is set by the general state of morality, knowledge, and common agreement.

It is, then, possible for government to take a man's life, qualify his liberty, regulate his property, direct his search for happiness—even forbid all anti-social outward manifestations of the inner drives of conscience—if this is done in fulfillment of a contract and in pursuit of known laws. The constitution and laws of every free state must recognize and protect man's natural rights. Whatever restrictions government places upon the free exercise of these rights must result from his freely given consent. The liberty that man retains is then properly styled "civil," or, if clearly recognized in fundamental law, "constitutional."

VI. In addition to those rights believed to be natural and unalienable, these derivative rights are the possession or aspiration of all men living under free government: the freedoms of speech, press, assembly, and petition; civil supremacy; representation and free elections; jury trial and attendant judicial safeguards. The first four are not only individual rights but social necessities, conditions as essential to the operation of free government as to the happiness of free men. The last two, representation and jury trial, are not only rights but the means of defending all other rights. In order to enjoy and defend their natural liberties a people need not adopt an exact imitation of the English legislative and judicial pattern, but the solid foundation of all free government is some form of equal representation and impartial trial. As to civil supremacy, this means simply that whatever regular armies must be raised for defense are to be subject at all times to legislative control. It means also that the right of a free citizen to be protected against military power and supremacy carries with it a correlative duty: to serve in a well-regulated militia, to combine the characters of citizen and soldier.

VII. Government—that is to say, good government—is a free association of free and equal men for certain well-defined purposes. It is not a necessary evil for which men can blame their moral insufficiencies, but a necessary blessing for which they can thank wise providence. Government is essential to the happiness of men, for only through the collective techniques that it provides can they order their relations with one another and do for themselves what they cannot do as individuals or in family groups.

Government is both a natural and mechanistic institution. It is natural in the sense that it is founded in the necessities of human nature: Man, a social and political animal, cannot exist without its protection and encouragement. It is mechanistic in the sense that he and his equal fellows have some control over the structure and complete control over its personnel. Though men are forced into government by their wants, they enter it on terms satisfactory to their interests and respectful of human nature. Good government is the result of a voluntary contract, which is another way of saying that good government is based on the consent of the governed.

VIII. The principle of consent, which is made visible in the contract, is the key to the problem of political obligation, the problem that forces men to ask such questions as: Why do we submit to the compulsions of government? By what authority does government bind us with positive laws? How can we call ourselves free if we are subject to a concentration of power that can restrict our liberty, deprive us of our property, even take away our lives? The answer is that men obey government because they have consented to obey it. Through the original contract they have exchanged allegiance and obedience for protection and peace. They have agreed to certain well-defined restrictions on their natural freedom as part of a scheme for securing the rest of that freedom against the whims and jealousies of the men with whom they live. At the same time, they have agreed to representative institutions, notably the legislative assembly and jury of peers, through which they can continue to consent to necessary restrictions on liberty and property. Government, the community organized for political purposes, can restrict men's liberty, deprive them of their property, even take away their lives, because it does all this with their original and continuing consent. The power of government to do these things is not intrinsic; it is derived from the free consent of the people it governs. In short, the answer to this troublesome series of questions is simply that the only valid obligation to obey government is self-obligation. The contract is therefore as much a logical justification as an historical explanation of the existence and authority of the political community.

The problem of sovereignty is of little concern to men with a sound grasp of the origin and nature of government. Sovereignty in the sense of supreme, irresistible, uncontrolled authority does not exist in free government and ought not exist in any government. Whatever rights or attributes of sovereignty government may exercise are the free and revocable grant of the people. And even the people, in whom sovereignty rests if it rests anywhere on earth, must be guided and restricted by the laws of nature in exercising their original political authority. They may not commission rulers to do what they may not do themselves: act in defiance of the laws of nature or in derogation from the rights of man.

IX. The purpose of society is to extend to each man in it, in return for his talents and exertions, the benefits of the strength, skills, and benevolence of the other men with whom he is associated. The purpose of government is to protect men in the enjoyment of their natural liberty, secure their persons and property against violence, remove obstructions to their pursuit of happiness, help them to live virtuous, useful lives, and in general preserve the largest degree of natural equality consistent with the welfare of the community and the implications of natural liberty. Neither government nor society, nor any third entity called the state, has any purpose of its own. Although it is proper to say that government exists for the safety, welfare, and happiness of the community, the community itself is nothing more than the individuals who make it up.

For this reason, it is not a dangerous thing to consider government an inherently good, even divine institution. Government can be safely acknowledged a temporal blessing because, in terms of the power it wields, there is nothing inherent about it. Government is not an end in itself but the means to an end. Its authority is the free and revocable grant of the men who have promised conditionally to submit to it. Its organs, however ancient and august, are instruments that free men have built and free men can alter or even abolish. Government can be arbitrary, corrupt, oppressive, wicked—but not if men are conscious of its origin, purpose, proper limits, and source of authority. Tyranny is not government but an abuse of government. True government is a good, natural, necessary institution ordained by providence to serve man's higher earthly purposes.

X. Under normal operating conditions of free society and constitutional government, representation and jury trial form the last and firmest line of defense against arbitrary power. When circumstances are abnormal, when this line of defense is irreparably breached, the people may resort to the great right of resistance. Government is divine, an ordinance of God, but governors are human, deriving all power from the consent of the governed. When rulers flout the terms under which they were granted this power, the people are placed in a position where they may, rather must, act to restore ordered liberty.

The right of resistance is the last refuge of a whole people unable to protect their lives, liberties, and properties by normal constitutional methods; it cannot be stretched to justify the *coup d'état* of a militant minority dedicated to the building of a new order. The people have a duty to be peaceful and law-abiding, and history demonstrates that they can be counted on never to resist except under overriding compulsion and to temper their methods to the nature and degree of oppression. The only possible outcome of a full reversion of power to the people is a new contract with new rulers under new terms of reciprocal obedience and protection. God granted men the right of resistance to help them preserve orderly government, not to induce them to fly from the tyranny of arbitrary power to the tyranny of no power at all. In short, resistance, the extreme form of which is revolution, is not so much the right as the solemn, unpleasant duty of a betrayed people.

XI. There is no one form of government good for all men at all times. Different communities may adopt different political systems yet reach the same level of liberty, prosperity, and happiness. A constitution is to be judged not by its logic or symmetry but by its ability to fulfill the great purposes for which all good governments are instituted. Yet if men are entirely free to adopt whatever form they desire, history and reason teach that most successful governments have exhibited the same characteristics and organs. Some structural rules for good government are:

1. Government must be plain, simple, and intelligible. The common sense of the common man should be able to comprehend its structure and functioning. Too often have governments been made unnecessarily complicated by elites or tyrants bent on enslaving the mass of the people.

2. Government must be republican, that is to say, representative and non-hereditary. Not only is simple democracy—government by the people directly—impractical in any community larger than a New England town or Swiss canton; history demonstrates that representatives of the people, wise men chosen by the community and accountable to it, make more sensible day-to-day decisions

than the people themselves. At the same time, there is no reason why these wise men, or one particular wise man as head of state, should occupy positions of decision by accident of birth. A virtuous, alert, liberty-loving people have no need of a king or hereditary aristocracy. They do have need of gifted, accountable leaders.

3. Government must be kept as near to the people as possible, chiefly through frequent elections and rotation-in-office. Frequent elections based on equal representation are the one sure means of keeping rulers responsible, of reminding them that they are servants not masters of the people. Rotation, which is secured by constitutional provisions forbidding indefinite re-eligibility, is an equally sure check against insolence in office. Another method of keeping government near to the people is, of course, to insist that they never delegate any task to government that they can do just as well for themselves.

4. Government must be constitutional, an empire of laws and not of men. The discretion and whim of all those in power must be reduced to the lowest level consistent with effective operation of the political machinery. The rule of law demands the existence of a written constitution, to be acknowledged and administered as a law superior to the acts of the legislature, decrees of the judiciary, and ordinances of the executive. It demands, too, the inclusion in this constitution of a specific declaration of natural and civil rights. Only thus can liberty be secured against defections of weak rulers and designs of strong. A true constitution has three sound claims to obedience and even veneration: It is the command of the people, an original compact expressing their unalienable sovereignty; the handiwork of the wisest men in the community; and an earthly expression of the eternal principles of the law

of nature. And a true constitution is a constant reminder that the only good government is limited government—limited in purpose, competence, and duration.

5. The one organ essential to free government is a representative legislature. The basic function of this organ—to serve as instrument of consent through which the people tax and restrict themselves—is evidence of its intrinsic character. Free government is difficult without an executive or judiciary; it is impossible without a representative assembly.

6. The fact of legislative primacy does not mean, however, that full, unchecked authority should be lodged in the representative assembly. The most successful and trustworthy governments are those in which the totality of political power is divided among three separate branches: a legislature, preferably bicameral; an executive, preferably single; and a judiciary, preferably independent. In turn, these branches should be held in position by a system of checks and balances. Divided and balanced government is something of a retreat from the principle that government must be plain, simple, and intelligible. A unified government—a one-chambered, unrestrained assembly—would certainly be easier to understand. Yet the advantages to be gained from separation and balance far outweigh those to be gained from union. Liberty rather than authority, protection rather than power, delay rather than efficiency must be the prime concern of constitution-makers. Balanced government, which leads to rule by a persistent and undoubted majority, is most likely to strike the proper balance between liberty and authority.

XII. Government in a free state is properly the concern of all those who have an attachment to the community.

The right to vote, as well as to hold office, should be limited to men who have an evident stake-in-society—first, because they alone can make competent, responsible, uncorrupted judgments; second, because they alone have the right to consent to laws regulating or restricting the use of property. Participation in public affairs through voting and office-holding is not so much a right as a privilege and duty. This is one instance in which natural equality must give way to the dictates of a well-ordered society. The burden of proof remains, however, on those who would restrict the suffrage: A man who pays taxes or owns a small amount of property would seem to have demonstrated sufficient attachment to the community. The laws should make it possible for any man, however lowly his beginnings, to work his way to first-class citizenship.

XIII. It takes more than a perfect plan of government to preserve ordered liberty. Something else is needed, some moral principle diffused among the people to strengthen the urge to peaceful obedience and hold the community on an even keel. The wisest of political philosophers speak of three possibilities: fear, honor, virtue. There can be little doubt which of these is essential to free government. Such government rests on a definite moral basis: a virtuous people. Men who are virtuous may aspire to liberty, prosperity, and happiness; men who are corrupt may expect slavery, adversity, and sorrow. In addition to such recognized virtues as wisdom, justice, temperance, courage, honesty, and sincerity, these may be singled out as attitudes or traits of special consequence for a free republic: the willingness to act morally without compulsion, love of liberty, public spirit and patriotism, official incorruptibility, and industry and frugality. Men who display these qualities are the raw materials of free government. Without such men, in low places as well as high, free government cannot possibly exist. Hortatory religion, sound education, honest government, and a simple, preferably agrarian economy can all help produce a people sufficiently virtuous to govern themselves. The task of political science is to discover the virtues that lead to free government and the form of government that leads men to virtue. That form of government is best which produces the greatest number of good, free, happy men. The best of all possible governments will be popular, limited, divided, balanced, representative, republican, responsible, constitutional—and virtuous.

To this summary one might also add a short catalogue of the major characteristics of Revolutionary political thought, a catalogue that reads:

Libertarianism—it placed man rather than the community at the center of political speculation, emphasizing his rights, his happiness, and his power to make and unmake government.

Optimism—it chose to stress the good and equal in men rather than the evil and unequal.

Tough-mindedness—it refused to carry this optimism to extravagant lengths and insisted on calling attention to pitfalls in the way of free government.

Idealism—it set out goals for all mankind that few men, even Americans, could hope to attain in their lives on earth.

Pragmatism—it tempered this idealism about ends with a refusal to be doctrinaire about means.

Morality—it insisted that free government, and therefore human liberty, is essentially a problem in practical ethics.

Perhaps the most remarkable characteristic of this system of political ideas was its deep-seated conservatism. However radical the principles of the Revolution may have seemed to the rest of the world, in the minds of the colonists they were thoroughly preservative and respectful of the past. Indeed, for generations to come Americans would be conservatives at home and radicals abroad. The explanation of this paradox lies in a decisive fact of history: By 1765 the colonies had achieved a society more open, an economy more fluid, a religion more humane, and a government more constitutional than anything Europeans would know for years to come. Americans had secured and were ready to defend a condition of freedom that other liberty-minded men could only hope for in the distant future or plot for in the brutal present. The political principles of the American Revolution, in contrast to those of the French Revolution, were not designed to make the world over. The world—at least the American corner of it—had already been made over as thoroughly as any sensible man could expect. Americans had never known or had long since begun to abandon feudal tenures, a privilege-ridden economy, centralized and despotic government, religious intolerance, and hereditary stratification. Their goal therefore was simply to consolidate, then expand by cautious stages, the large measure of liberty and well-being that was part of their established way of life. More than 150 years ago Americans took up their unique role of the world's most conservative radicals, the world's most sober revolutionists. They, like their descendants, spurned the attractive nostrums of both the Enlightenment and Romanticism for a philosophy dedicated realistically to personal liberty within a context of communal stability.

Were we to judge even the most lucid and subtle of Revolutionary thinkers by standards usually applied to such as Aristotle, Hobbes, or Hegel, we should have to write a rather strong critique of the principles, organization, and mode of expression of their political thought. Not only were they guilty of all the sins against logic, history, and psychology committed by the long line of philosophers dedicated to natural law and the compact; they were open to reproach on other counts. Certainly it would not be difficult to make a case for each of these criticisms of the Revolutionary school:

Mediocrity—it failed to produce, at least during the Revolution itself, a single thinker or book worthy of universal attention.

Superficiality—it refused to probe more than a few inches beneath the surface of such problems as obligation and the origin of government.

Lack of originality—it accepted almost without reservation the most universal of political theories and added few refinements or doctrines of its own.

Confusion—it answered the hard question, Is government natural or mechanistic in origin? by insisting that it was both.

Hypocrisy—out of the mouths of slave-holders the world heard the passionate scriptures of natural justice and equality.

Yet how damning are these criticisms? Are all schools of political thought to be judged mediocre and superficial if they cannot produce an Aristotle or *Contrat Social?* The political thought of the Revolution was the faith of a people in hot pursuit of liberty rather than the dialectic of an intellectual elite detached from the stress of affairs, and it should be judged as such by intellectual historians. Moreover, John Adams and George Mason might well ask their critics whether the Massachusetts Constitution and Virginia Declaration of Rights were not among the world's most memorable triumphs in applied political theory. The charge of intellectual confusion is impossible to refute but at least some of this confusion may be written off to the activist careers of the great spokesmen of the Revolution.

Two points can be made in rebuttal to the alleged lack of originality in Revolutionary thought: First, the colonists were, as I have insisted repeatedly, conscious traditionalists. In proclaiming the doctrines of natural law and the contract, they held fast to their colonial and English heritage. Not indifference or poverty of intellect, but pride and a sense of history persuaded the colonists to take their stand at the end of the heroic line of Protagoras, Cicero, Aquinas, Hooker, Locke, and Burlamaqui. Second, we should not forget how rare a thing it is for a man or school to make a genuinely original contribution to political thought. The Revolutionists would appear to have done their share by providing theoretical justification of written constitutions and bills of rights. Through these noble instruments they converted the contract into a working principle of constructive statesmanship.

The mark of hypocrisy must not be stamped too impetuously upon the philosophers of the Revolution, for slavery was an inherited fact of infinite complexity that most of them looked forward confidently to ending in a generation or two. Indeed, the intense popularity of natural law and rights accelerated the movement toward abolition of slavery, or at least suppression of the slave trade, to a noticeable degree. Most petitions, letters, and pamphlets that demanded emancipation labeled slavery, in the words of James Otis, "the most shocking violation of the law of nature" and called blunt attention to the moral inconsistency of legislatures that proclaimed natural rights yet failed to repeal their slave codes. The moral case against slavery had more appeal than the practical or economic in these years of concern for liberty and equality. An anonymous author spoke for tens of thousands of colonists when he wrote in Rind's *Virginia Gazette* in 1767:

> As freedom is unquestionably the birthright of all mankind, Africans as well as Europeans, to keep the former in a state of slavery is a constant violation of that right, and therefore of justice.

In conclusion, we may well ask: By what tests is the historian of ideas to measure the excellence of a political philosophy? By its conformity to truth? By its logic, precision, profundity, and symmetry? By its purpose? By the past on which it draws and the future to which it in turn communicates? By its influence on the world of political reality?

The truth of the political principles of the American Revolution is for philosophers to ponder, and while they ponder they would do well to remember three oft-forgotten facts: The Declaration of Independence was written in 1776, not 1861 or 1932 or 1963; the men who signed it were entirely sincere, never doubting for a moment that the truths announced in the first paragraph were "self-evident"; the men who wrote it—Jefferson, Adams, Franklin—had a unique grasp of the relationship between ideal and reality in the processes of successful self-government. As to the second test, no one, least of all the Revolutionists themselves, would deny that their principles could easily have been rendered more logical, precise, profound, and symmetrical. The plea of the defense is that these men were makers of history with a flair for speculative generalization, not philosophers in single-minded search of ultimate truth.

The philosophy of the Revolution was earnest faith rather than ordered theory. Would it not therefore be fitting and honorable to judge it by the last three of the tests we have established? Judged in this manner, it stands forth as one of the most noble and influential of all political philosophies. Its purpose was liberty and happiness for all men everywhere. The past on which it drew was that of Locke rather than Hobbes, of the *Vindiciae contra tyrannos* rather than *The Prince*, of Chrysippus rather than Thrasymachus. The future to which it communicated was constitutional democracy rather than the omnipotent state. And as for its influence on the world of political reality, it justified and inspired the makers of the greatest of revolutions, teaching them to build the new temple of ordered liberty even as they tore down the old one of imperial dependence. Abraham Lincoln caught the true meaning of the principles of the Revolution when he wrote in 1859 of the document in which they were recommended "to the opinions of mankind":

All honor to Jefferson—to the man, who, in the concrete pressure of a struggle for national independence by a single people, had the coolness, forecast, and capacity to introduce into a merely revolutionary document an abstract truth, applicable to all men and all times, and so to embalm it there that today and in all coming days it shall be a rebuke . . . to the very harbingers of reappearing tyranny.

All honor, too, to the Adamses, the Lees, Wilson, Paine, Franklin, Otis, Dickinson, Parsons, Hamilton, and "the black Regiment" of preachers, who worked with a will to create the political thought of the American Revolution, still the mightiest and most convincing "rebuke" ever delivered to the "harbingers of reappearing tyranny."

Index

Adams, Amos, 9

Adams, John, 6, 46, 68, 71;
  writings, 10, 15, 30, 35;
  quoted, 15-16, 23, 43-44,
    53-54, 68, 128-130,
    134, 149, 197-198, 209-
    210, 210-211;
  political thought, 88, 97,
    103, 106, 107, 131,
    133, 135, 163-164, 166,
    171, 178, 179, 202;
  constitutional thought,
    170, 182, 188, 195;
  theory of British power
    over colonies, 23, 29,
    154;
  as representative political
    thinker, 196-197, 231;
  on education, 16, 207-208

Adams, Samuel, 43, 200;
  writings, 10-11, 14, 37,
    55-57;
  quoted, 22-23, 45, 85, 99,
    111, 126, 131, 204-205;
  political thought, 130,

162, 165-166, 175, 199-
  200

Addison, Joseph, 68

agrarianism, 208-209, 228

Allen, John, 9, 35, 66, 141-
  142, 155-156

Allen, Thomas, 9, 98, 182

almanacs, 12

America, destiny of, 49-51,
  101-102, 172-173

Ames, Nathaniel, 12, 70,
  191, 200-201, 204, 210

Anglicanism, 9

anti-slavery sentiment, 232

Aquinas, St. Thomas, 66,
  231

Aristotle, 65, 66

Articles of Confederation,
  155

assembly, freedom of, 121,
  124-125

Bancroft, Edward, 21, 92,
  201

Barnard, Edward, 9

235